Steep Passages

A world-wide eco-adventurer unlocks nature's spiritual truths

Steep Passages

A world-wide eco-adventurer unlocks nature's spiritual truths

DAVID LEE DROTAR

Brookview Press
901 Western Road
Castleton-on-Hudson
New York 12033
www.brookviewpress.com

Published 2002 by Brookview Press, 901 Western Road, Castleton-on-Hudson, New York 12033. Copyright © 2002 by David Lee Drotar. All rights reserved. No part of this book may be reproduced, stored in a retrieval system, or transmitted in any form or by any means, electronic, mechanical, recording or otherwise, without the prior written permission of the publisher.

Manufactured in the United States of America.

Library of Congress Control Number 2002090429

ISBN 0-9707649-0-1

Cover illustration and book design by Dominic Poon

contents

the soul of a traveler

Most of the world travelers I meet have two things in common. They're intelligent, reflective beings and they've always had wanderlust. They look beneath the surface of their surroundings, never content to accept the obvious. And, they're never content to stay home.

I met Garik just as he was about to embark on a two-year, round-the-world bike tour. This was his most ambitious cycling tour, but certainly not his first. A college professor who bills himself on the internet as the "cycling scholar," he had lived, taught and traveled in such diverse places as Switzerland and Siberia, and published his articles on economic theory in the *New York Times* and other periodicals. Now he would be hitting the road again, inching across four continents. As the world made its passage into the new millennium, his bike would bring him into the midst of hurricanes, killer bees, earthquakes and military coups. He would contract a rare form of malaria.

My first thought was *why?* This guy, like myself, was in his forties – generation Advil. But shame on me. I knew why. It was simply part of his psyche to explore. He didn't really have any choice in the matter, only the mechanism. When I was asking about his physical route around the globe, I should have been asking what route his life had taken to get here.

I had that chance when he returned on schedule, two years later, just as he had planned. I learned, not surprisingly, that Garik had run away from home when he was eight years old.

"I had longings to leave home and see what was over the next hill for as far back as I can remember," he recalls of his childhood in the Berkshire mountains of western Massachusetts. At this same time he had developed an intense interest in movie stars. Knowing that they lived in California, he decided he would try to find one. He knew about roads and signs and had a good sense of direction. So, he reasoned, all he had to do was walk to the west coast.

"I just started walking one afternoon," he says, "out Route 20 to this road in Hancock called Central Berkshire Boulevard, and turned south..."

Unfortunately, young Garik hadn't yet fully grasped the concepts of time and distance. Only when it became too dark and cold to continue did he realize he had made a big mistake. The adventure ended without tragedy when the police found him along the Massachusetts Turnpike and returned him safely to his frantic parents.

My own initiation into the club of travelers was not as predictable but maybe no less insane. I was twenty-three years old when I decided to take my first trip. I was always interested in nature and the environment, and was beginning to develop an awareness of other cultures. Having never traveled further from upstate New York than to Pennsylvania, I made a five-week trip into the jungles of Venezuela.

Maybe because of the difficulty of traveling alone in an undeveloped country without knowing the language, I grew up a lot during that single month of my life and came away with a better environmental and cultural sensitivity. Over the next few decades I traveled much more and always had a curiosity about the lives of the people I encountered along the way and how they got to where they were. Like the apparent fate that draws the Gariks of the world to explore its furthest corners, there was a certain inevitability about their life forces — although the individual paths they took through life varied greatly.

The passages that we navigate never seem easy at the time. After the attacks on America we all came to realize very emphatically that the world doesn't have the same boundaries anymore. But I've long believed that there are certain universalities that cross borders, cultures, ages and genders. I've compiled a group of some of my favorite travel essays that I've written and published in recent years. Wherever you are in life right now, I hope reading them inspires you to reflect upon or forge your own steep passages.

winter

I. steep passage

Pale morning sunlight poked seductively through breaks in thick clouds as the sleek, high-speed gondola purred quietly along its ribbon to the sky. Sitting comfortably inside, I watched my skis, attached to the outside of the red cubicle, whiz past the barren trees.

"This your first run today?" I asked the two young men seated across from me.

"Nope. We've come down already." The first guy balanced a snowboard between his boots. His heavy stubble told me that he had just rolled out of bed and headed directly for the slopes. Looks like me in the seventies as I would dash to an 8:00 Psych 101 class, I thought.

"What's it like?" I asked.

"New powder at the top. Awesome run."

I noticed season lift tickets strapped around their arms in protective plastic cases. "You guys ski instructors?"

"Nah. We work in the ski dorm," he answered.

"College students?"

"Uh, sort of post college…" the second guy joined in. "We don't know what we want to do yet."

"Yeah, ski bums." Snowboard smirked. "We get a season pass and hang out for a while."

"Hey, there's nothing wrong with that," I said. "Now's the time to do it." I watched the base lodge grow smaller and smaller.

"How about you?" the second guy asked.

"I'm a writer. I'm doing a ski story on Stowe and Smugglers'."

"That's cool." Snowboard approved.

The sun grew brighter and I gaped at the incredible incandescent swirling patchwork of blue sky and clouds that scraped the eye-level 4,000-foot peaks and cast everchanging silvery shadows on the valley below. The gondola slowed to a crawl and wedged itself into the tracks of the summit station. The doors automatically slid open, Murphy Brown elevator-style to release the compartment's odd combination of characters onto an alpine stage.

Snowboard stepped out and his friend grabbed a pair of racing skis from the rack. "Have a good run, sir," he said with a brand of politeness I found annoying. They saw me as their elder, someone to whom a respectful tone is due. So, maybe I'm not the scruffy vagabond anymore. But I'm not old.

We trudged onto the crunchy packed powder with our clunky ski boots and stepped into our respective sliding equipment.

"Thanks. You too," I said, pulling my fuzzy Turtle Fur neck piece up around my chin like the Bazooka Joe character from the bubble gum comics of my youth.

Snowboard and Company bolted gracefully down the mountain while I clung tentatively to the edge like a frayed piece of Velcro ready to be ripped loose at any moment. I was at that awkward stage in my skiing development – not a beginner but not quite good enough to navigate the intermediate trails without a tumble now and then.

There was a moment of hesitation – no, fear – as I looked at the steep pitch lying below me. I'm told that even experienced racers feel this trepidation every time they start out. I found little solace in the thought that Italy's World Cup racer, Alberto Tomba might be suppressing the same flutter before he hurtled down the slalom run in Stowe's Annual World Military Ski Championships in March. After all, his warm-up probably consisted of a couple runs over the double black diamond "Nosedive" trail.

I pushed off and felt the rush of bitterly cold air against my cheeks. But I warmed quickly as I gently swooshed back and forth over the wide "Gondolier" trail, retracing the route we had just ascended to the crest of Mount Mansfield, Vermont's highest peak. My skis danced over the glittering snow, the meticulous grooming reminding me that, even here, I was never far from the amenities for which Stowe is renowned. From the five-course luncheon in a mountain-top restaurant to the ski-up deck and cafe featuring freshly baked muffins and croissants, I might just as well have been in Austria as northern New England.

If the slope-side accoutrements provided a few creature comforts with a quaint international flair, Stowe village was a cosmopolitan skier's vision carried to the limit. Could the singing von Trapp family who settled the area in the 1940s have predicted their simple lodge would spawn the proliferation of the imitation-German inns, restaurants and gift shops that lined the main road through town? The Salzburg Inn, Winterhaus, Romy's Alpen Haus, Timberholm Inn, The Stowehof Inn, The Yodler Inn... Was it a parody run amok? Even McDonald's had gone arch-less in Stowe.

I gently slid into the base elevation where I hooked up with several other journalists and Kris, Stowe's public relations coordinator, who was taking us on a "Mountain Tour" on skis. Bright, bubbly and blond, she would not have been out of place hosting a network morning show. And with a slight twenty-something naivete that her Ivy-league education couldn't quite erase, she was the personification of Stowe's appeal.

"So, how'd you get into the PR business?" I wondered out loud, nudging my way past other skiers who might dare to sit between us on the four-person chair lift.

"I was a ski instructor," she said, beginning the typical story of transformation from suburban flatlander to mountaineer, that I was to hear repeated in varying versions during my stay. "When this job opened up, it gave me the chance to stay in the area year round."

The lift scooped us off the ground and we climbed open-air style to the summit, skis dangling from our feet, as Kris explained the steps Stowe was taking to win back the title "ski capital of the East." From the introduction of night skiing on lighted trails to computerized snow-making, it was obvious Stowe had the financial resources to compete.

Chilled from the brisk ride, we disembarked and our group assembled once more. Like a disjointed centipede, the skiing caravan wriggled its way down the "Toll Road" trail following our leader Kris in the distinctive "Stowe Host" shiny silver jacket. Lining the narrow trail, stunted spruce trees sported their own shimmering coats of frozen ice and snow.

"That's Spruce Peak over there," Kris pointed out, explaining the nighttime summer concerts held in the natural amphitheater. With hot stars performing in the off-season, Stowe could maintain its glitzy image and still have a broad-based appeal.

"And Smugglers' Notch is that way." The steep passage etched between mountains bore the same name as the ski resort that lay on the other side. During the summer, one could hike or drive through the notch, but the pass was closed in winter except to skiers who wished to traverse the two mountains.

We zigzagged down the rest of the "Toll Road" with a few more stops and a few spills along the way. Each time I picked myself up and pointed my skis downhill. I was going to explore Smugglers', to see what lay on the other side.

Exploration, however, wasn't the intent of the early nineteenth century opportunists operating on the other side of the law. With Thomas Jefferson's 1806 embargo on goods from England, the notch formed the ideal passageway for smugglers to transport illicit cloth, food and glass from Canada into Vermont and the rest of the United States. During prohibition in the twentieth century, the notch functioned as an illegal conduit for alcohol. Recognizing the historical significance of the pass, in 1933 Rand McNally adopted the colloquial designation and officially used the term Smugglers' Notch on its map of the area.

*   *   *

"I'm convinced that skiing is totally alien to the human survival mechanism." These weren't the words I wanted to hear, especially coming from the Assistant Ski School Director.

Sherm White plugged the SyberVision videotape into the VCR and the television flickered. A stylish skier with a fluorescent triangle emblazoned on his jacket created artistic, fluid movements back and forth across the screen. He looked like a highway yield sign reincarnated to a better life.

"Watch the triangle," Sherm directed.

Back and forth. Back and forth. Soft piano notes played in the background.

"Notice the tip of the triangle."

Back and forth. Back and forth. The motion was hypnotic.

"Now watch his skis slide together as he makes the turn."

Back and forth. Back and forth. I understood why they called this visual imprinting. I'd be seeing this damn triangle during my sleep.

"OK, let's get in some quality sliding time."

We spilled out of the office and took the two-person chair lift up Morse Mountain. I quizzed him about his background. A forty-ish, outdoorsy kind of guy, Sherm had trained to be a lawyer before coming to Smugglers' twenty years ago. It was harder imagining him in a three-piece suit before a judge than it was a flannel shirt while timber harvesting on family acreage during the off-ski season. But it wasn't hard to see how the seemingly divergent life goals were the skiing profession's eventual gain. He had a comfortable sense of where he was in the universe, that my middle years could appreciate.

The lift reached the top and our skis skimmed the small hump in the terrain next to the attendant's station. The chair pulled itself from my body as I stood up and slid away.

"Go ahead," Sherm called. "I'll follow you. I want to watch your form."

I turned down the "Garden Path" trail. Imagining myself inside a big triangle, I skied back and forth down the trail.

"Good! Stop here." Sherm magically appeared at my side. "I want to point out a few things."

His easy, non-threatening manner made me eager to hear his thoughts. He praised the things I was doing right and then gently made some suggestions for improvement. We skied a little bit further down the trail and then he offered additional pointers. Eventually we arrived back at the lift. We repeated the scenario several times that afternoon. By the end of the day, I felt that I was a better skier – a claim that I wouldn't have made after spending a week in posh St. Moritz, Switzerland several years ago.

With over two hundred ski instructors, Smugglers' program for hiring and training personnel seemed gargantuan. A four-day job interview, including two days spent in a team-centered ropes adventure course, kicked off the selection process. In addition to technical skiing expertise, the key to a successful ski instructor was obviously an ability to work with people's personalities and build trust.

And if these qualities were important for teaching adult skiers, they must be critical for introducing children to the sport, I mused as I lay in bed that night. I'd be learning first-hand about the children's program tomorrow. Outside the cozy Nordland condominium, heavy rain blew against the patio doors. I closed my eyes. But I didn't see sunny blue skies. I didn't see powdery trails. I saw fluorescent triangles whirling across icy slopes...

The next morning, a raw chill filled the air as I donned my skis and slid over to the Morse Mountain lift to meet Peter Ingvoldstad, the Director of the children's ski school. With their instructor towering over them, a class of pre-schoolers inched along the roped-off lift line. Peter conferred with the instructor for a few moments.

Then he turned to me and asked, "Do you mind taking a kid up with you?"

"Uh, no. I guess not." I didn't know exactly what I was agreeing to, but it didn't sound too complicated.

Before I could back down, I found myself sitting down on the two-person chair lift while the lift attendant hoisted a tiny girl clad in a fuzzy pink outfit onto the space next to me. Without stopping, the chair rose up the mountain.

"I'm not afraid," she announced boldly. That was good, because I was scared enough for her. Scared that she might slip out of the chair. I held my ski pole across the front of her as an adjunct precaution to the safety bar. The chair swayed in the wind.

"Sometimes when I get to the edge of the hill, I get scared," she suddenly confessed. Her tiny pink mittens held the safety bar.

"Oh? Then what do you do?"

"I just go. Then I'm not scared anymore."

Hmmm. A good philosophy. Why didn't I think of that?

"How old are you?"

"Four."

"That's a nice age." I glanced backward to see other little children riding up.

"That's my friend behind us," she said.

"What's her name?" I asked.

"I don't know. We have fun."

The chair approached the mid-station and I cautiously lifted the safety bar and removed my protective ski pole. As we passed the hut, the attendant reached out his arms to pick up the girl, and in one continuous motion sent the tiny pink snow bunny down the incline. I continued on to the final station.

At the top of Morse Mountain, I met Peter again, as well as a fellow writer, Willis, and his nine-year-old daughter, Lisa. We made a quick run down the slope where the grooming machines had admirably performed their nightly routine, transforming the crusty surface into granular, sugar-like particles.

We played "helicopter" moving our arms above our heads like spinning blades, and "Geronimo" diving from our imaginary aircraft. Both games were designed to isolate various body motions and translate them into precise skiing maneuvers.

"Even before we come outdoors, we work with images," Peter explained the innovative ski school's approach. A baby-boomer with three young children of his own, he referenced classic children's books like *The Runaway Bunny* by Margaret Wise Brown.

"We read stories to the kids and pretend we're the characters." I could see that there was still a child underneath the inevitable crow's-feet and thickening midsection.

Up the same lift again, this time we skied down the "Midway" trail, a crossover path designed to take us to another lift – and another mountain. At the end of the line we found ourselves atop Madonna Mountain, but unlike the aging sex symbol, the name's religious reverence became obvious when we teetered at the brink of "Father Bob's" trail.

Peter, Willis, Lisa and I cast off. The grooming machines hadn't reached this trail, and with the previous night's cycle of rain and arctic blast, the surface was slick. Slow and deliberate, Willis pointed the tips of his skis together and wedged his way back and forth across the steep, but wide, trail.

Out of control, I shot past him.

Landing a few hundred feet below with my limbs arranged in a gelatinous jumble, I looked up. I saw a wall of ice. Down the side of the wall – in full control – Peter was skiing backwards guiding a future Olympian to less intimidating terrain. Her confidence unshaken, Lisa proudly joined her father, I buried my bruised ego, and we all continued down the trail.

From the ski bums savoring one last winter in the mountains before moving to the cities to earn a living, to a mid-lifer carving his niche in the sport he loved, at that point I realized the route between Stowe and Smugglers' Notch was indeed a steep passage. Life's transitions are sometimes icy, often scary. The more we think about them, the more difficult they seem. How do we get through them?

As the pink snow bunny would say, we just go.

2. convolutions

I float over the frozen earth's cerebral folds. Like neurons reaching into the brain's recesses, rivers entwine themselves into the furrowed landscape of these things called the Rockies. My aircraft descends and I am caught in their enigmatic psyche.

0 m.p.h. Large snowflakes fall gently and steadily through the pungent, blue haze hanging over the old Texaco sign at the mountain lodge's snowmobile fueling station. I sit atop the sleek black Arctic Cat whose engine purrs in unison with the others in our pack. Back East, I'd hear the distant buzz of an occasional snowmobile after a storm. But they were the domain of isolated rural communities or teenaged speed demons.

I've never driven a "sled" before. I'm a wanderer, a hiker. I'm used to leisurely exploring trails, stopping frequently to gaze at a distant vista or examine a wildflower underfoot. This is winter, however, and the snow is deep in the mountains. The 600-inch average annual snowfall in Wyoming's Togwotee pass precludes such ramblings. On a snowmobile I could reach otherwise inaccessible places. Unencumbered by fatigue, I could go further and see more.

Our young guide, Mark, has dutifully instructed us in the use of the machines. I fiddle with the controls, not quite knowing what to think about this bourgeois mode of travel. Beneath the instrument panel's speedometer, odometer and tachometer, I flip a switch and through my insulated gloves I feel the soothing heat of the handlebar warmers.

10 m.p.h. I squeeze my right thumb, pressing the throttle to the handlebar, and listen to the engine rev. My feet tucked neatly into their cubbyholes on the running boards, I accelerate powerfully ahead. I move past an assortment of cars, trucks and four-wheel drive vehicles in the snow-packed parking lot.

We must cross the highway to reach the trail, and I await Mark's signal. When all is clear, I proceed gingerly across the snowless pavement, while trying to maintain enough momentum to ascend the slight hump created by the snowplows.

Our caravan chugs along the wide, groomed trail lined by evergreen boughs teetering under the weight of snowy globules. My machine bounces rhythmically over the hardened ridges and moguls carved into the frozen thoroughfare. Up and down, my thighs develop a posting motion in anticipation of each bump.

20 m.p.h. I squeeze the throttle tighter and steer my sled around a curve, gently leaning into the acceleration. The distant craggy Tetons cut swatches through the overcast sky ahead, and I am magically whisked from one light-bathed vista to the next. Effortlessly I climb higher and higher, coming to the crest of one knoll and immediately descending into its hidden abyss. I roll over miles of undulating terrain, my mind slurping in the wintry scenes one after another.

The day warms and the snow softens, even at 9,000 feet elevation. Pleased with the group's progress, Mark yells over the din of the engines, "OK, gang. Let's experience some of that famous Togwotee powder!"

We leave the security of hard-packed surfaces for looser footing. I zigzag through forested slopes, my sled wedged cozily into paths mere inches wider than the machine itself. With the runners pointed uphill and the other group members on my heels, I dare not stop. I cannot linger to examine the playful ceremony of light and shadows in the tree tops or the translucent frosty coatings of pine needles at eye level. But no matter. There is no lack of sensory stimulation as we press deeper into the mountains' cranial pathways.

30 m.p.h. Brisk, moist air pushes stale snowmobile exhaust fumes against my face in a paradoxical mixture. Refusing to blend with each other philosophically, if not chemically, each retains its own distinct identity. Yet without one, I do not perceive the other.

The trail breaks out of the forest and becomes more powdery. I traverse open hillsides, leaning uphill to prevent the machine's drive belt from losing its tenuous grip with the earth and starting a "rolldown." Soon we enter a hidden valley, buzzing our way across virgin snow fields. A mother moose nibbles the lower branches of an evergreen and we steer clear.

We frolic. Like an oversized *Fantasia* set, we make figure eights amongst each other, kicking up clouds of fluffy snow that glistens in the mid-day sun. I gun the engine, rising up the wall of the valley until there is no more power left, and then abruptly turning downhill for the roller-coaster descent.

40 m.p.h. On to our next destination, I brace myself with arms grasping the handlebars in an outstretched "Y" position. As if I had discovered a torturous new health club exercise, now my upper body moves in tandem with the jouncing metal.

I climb up the mountain in several stages. At the narrow, boulder-framed gateway to one of the level terraces, a porcupine waddles out to see who is raising the commotion in its private sphere. But we've got things to do and places to go, so we beam ourselves up to the next level.

Rising another thousand feet above our 10,000-foot perch, the Breccia cliffs halt any further advancement. Snowy caps stick to the jagged vermillion spikes, but we can not taste the bigger-than-life popsicles.

Never mind. We go to another vantage point. We fly down this mountain and up another, trying to outrun a sudden snow squall. Even the thrust of eighty-horsepower, liquid-cooled engines, however, is no match for the synaptic speed of transmission at the mountains' upper cortex. We're caught in a white-out and I trustingly follow the bouncing black dots scattered ahead of me in the swirling mass.

50 m.p.h. I cruise past the scorched remnants of vast tracts of lodgepole pine forests in Yellowstone National Park. Dodging the radar guns of rangers, I glide over the smooth, snow-packed straightaways opened to snowmobile traffic during the winter. The ride is effortless and I share the highway with roving bands of buffalo who have also discovered that there's an easier alternative to trudging through deep snow.

I pass through eerie thermal areas whose bubbling caldrons of water burn holes through the snow cover and fill the air with dense gray fog. Any imaginary visions of prehistoric creatures lurking among the steamy, shadowy silhouettes evaporate as quickly as the dew on my windshield. I'm off to the next site.

I stand among hundreds of booted, mittened people who have parked their sleds and wait for the hourly eruption of Old Faithful. The event is late from its predicted spouting time, but true to its name, the geyser eventually blows. Water bubbles from the cone-shaped mound and climbs higher and higher, forming a feathery plume that reaches a hundred feet into the air. After a few minutes, the water loses its oomph and the process reverses itself. Then, like a giant Harley rally, the throngs of spectators start their snowmobile engines in a deafening roar, and I shoot out onto the speedway.

60 m.p.h. Out of the park, we once again head into the back country where there is no speed limit. I blast through open meadows, powdery ribbons streaming from each side of my sled. I careen over a snow-laden wooden bridge, wondering what symphony the rock-strewn stream trickling beneath it might be playing. But I'll never know.

Sandwiched between the brilliantly white snowy landscape and the blue sky, lies a cloud layer. My sled climbs into it and suddenly the cool mist chills my face. My entire field of vision includes only the snowmobile ahead of me and blurry white streaks to my sides.

A half hour later, we poke through the top of the cloud. The sunlight that creates an iridescent, heavenly glow in the rising mist also hits my dark suit in a warm embrace. Is that a choir of angels wielding chain saws? We pause in a small clearing. In the distance lie the unscalable Breccia cliffs whose sight triggers Mark to remember a dream he had last night.

"I'm guiding a group of seniors at the top of that ridge," he says, "when one snowmobiler's runner slips off the edge."

To the other side of the clearing, beyond our line of sight, lies the taller Austin Peak, our destination. Explaining that we cannot stay together during this part of the trip, Mark verbally maps out the rest of the terrain. He expresses his pleasure with the group and his confidence that we can make the rest of the journey individually.

70 m.p.h. We space ourselves several minutes apart. When it is my turn, I squeeze the throttle all the way down and ascend the open hillside, constantly gaining speed. I enter another forest, deftly maneuvering the metal hulk side-to-side between looming tree trunks. My body jounces wildly as the machine bounces in and out of deeply corrugated troughs.

Never easing up on the throttle, I then enter a massive chute devoid of vegetation. Like a toy car trying to make its way up an icy bobsled run, I weave from side to side, feeling the tenuous hold that the belt has on the surface. But any loss of speed whatsoever would halt the gradual upward progress.

At the end of the chute I find myself staring into the depths of a huge snow bowl, as large as a sports stadium but rounded at the bottom. There are only two directions: straight down and then straight up. I swoop down one side, and as I near the bottom I give the engine all the juice it can take. It works. I climb out of the bowl and over the lip.

Swerving to avoid rocks that the wind has swept bare, I climb a few more hundred feet and I'm at the 11,500-foot summit. I shut off the engine. I've earned the right to gawk at the convoluted land lying below me in all directions. In one tidy package, I see all the peaks, all the hills, all the valleys through which I've just come.

80 m.p.h. I start the engine again and sprint back down the slope, at last comfortable with the knowledge that I've explored the inner cerebral recesses of the mountains – as well as my own.

3. journey through the ice

On the eve of an historic summit meeting between world leaders, I jumped into the sea.

It was the same body of water where a rosy-cheeked Boris Yeltsin took a dip to demonstrate his vigor to the outside world amid speculations of failing health. Today, in a hole cut into the frozen Baltic Sea across from the neighboring shores of Russia, I lay on my back and paddled. Snow swirled around me. Chunks of ice the size of frozen turkeys floated by.

Getting here had been an interesting journey…

THE REAL SANTA CLAUS

"Real Santa lives in FEEN-land," our sturdy Finnish leader, Ritva, assured my friends and me as we flew from Helsinki at the southern tip of Finland, to the Lapland region above the Arctic Circle. Like the other Finns I was to meet, her features and speech did not seem at all Scandinavian, but more reminiscent of my own eastern European ancestry. I thought of my animated Polish aunts who chattered away in the Cold War era of the sixties about bomb shelters and imminent Russian invasions.

Yet now I wondered if radiation released from the 1986 Chernobyl nuclear disaster might linger in the reindeer herds which grazed in its fallout path. The Laplanders depended on the animals for every part of their existence – reindeer meat and milk for food, hides for clothing and shelter. Even the bones and antlers were skillfully carved into useful items such as belts or gun powder holders.

Increasingly, the tourists who came in winter played more of a role in the economics of the frozen tundra. As I glided through sunny meadows on a one-person sleigh pulled by a single reindeer, I realized that the waste-not want-not lifestyle even pervaded Finnish folklore. Santa Claus wouldn't fuss with eight finicky personalities when one dependable employee could easily get the job done.

The real Santa, however, was caught in a curious time warp between aboriginal cultures and a new-millennium reality check that involved marketing reindeer meat and products to the rest of Finland and the world. It appeared that snowmobiles and four-wheel-drive vehicles were faster and more efficient in transporting members of the fifty-seven reindeer keeper associations across a "Lapland kilometer."

As easily as Finnish vodka flowed on a biting Arctic night, I moved from reindeer sleighing to dog sledding. At Harrinivan

Lomakyha, a hundred and fifty eager huskies warmed the day with puppy-like greetings of yelps, jumps, and cuddly nuzzles.

Looking the part of the pack leader, Köpi, the burly, bearded owner of the twenty-three-year-old business, answered my questions about the operation.

"The dogs we choose for team," he explained, "depend on individuals. Some personalities work better together than others." How true, I thought. Could international politics be too far removed from this principle?

Clinton and Yeltsin would be meeting in Finland next week to discuss NATO plans to consider several new states. Latvia, Lithuania and Estonia had applied for membership in the organization after spending fifty years as unwilling members of the former Soviet Union. Now it was Russia who objected to the possibilities of expansion.

I lowered myself into the sled and the driver released his foot from the grab bar that dug into the crusty snow. Immediately the sled moved under the power of the tugging canine team. The dogs worked in harmony as we silently glided over gentle hills and around curves. To my left, I saw the land drop gently to a frozen river – the border with the former "Kingdom of Sweden" to which Finland had belonged for six centuries before coming under the rule of czarist Russia. Soon the dogs returned to their home base where Köpi stood in mukluks and beaver hat, talking on his Finnish-made, state-of-the-art Nokia cell phone.

After a relaxing sauna and a night under a down comforter, I spent the next day exploring the snowy landscape under my own power. The barren *tunturi* that rose from the rolling tundra were not majestic like the Rockies or awe-inspiring like the Alps. But rather their comforting pinkish glow during the two-hour Arctic sunrise was like a hug that assures a toddler of love before he tests his way in the real world. Had I met a vicious, child-eating *staalo* along my route, surely I could have negotiated a settlement.

My arduous snowshoe hike to the 1,000-foot summit of Keskinenlaki Tunturi continued to offer mixed signals of danger and comfort. Throughout a rapidly changing meteorological gamut of fog, snow and brilliant sunshine, I plodded over the cake-like surface, occasionally sinking waist deep into the snow. I lunched in a sheltered glade under towering spruces, and hiked along open ridges where I braced myself against the wind. At the summit, I gazed at the glistening white stage lying before me. This theater encompassed the whole world and the actors were the global community.

But that night I was hypnotically drawn from the warmth of my hotel room to the frigid outdoors once again. Propped against a snow drift, I stared up at the sky. Comet Hale-Bopp streaked across the horizon as shooting stars hurled themselves like random *Star Wars* missiles. Superimposed over the heavens, a display of Northern Lights danced like a shimmering curtain pulled across the earth. I wondered what kind of drama I would find when the curtain opened...

Weatherproofed with layers of sweaters, socks and face masks under our one-piece wind suits, my friends and I climbed onto our snowmobiles and revved the engines. Leaving the city of Kemi behind us, we buzzed over the frozen Gulf of Bothnia on the Baltic Sea in search of the icebreaker *Sampo*. Squeezing the throttle while my partner, Florence, held onto my waist, I recalled the story she had told me earlier that day. Her four-year-old granddaughter had taken her to school as a show-and-tell item.

"This is my grandmother," the little girl said. "She doesn't bake cookies."

"Oh." One of her friends stared in amazement. "What does she do?"

"I don't know, but she's not home very much."

The sunny skies that had lured us onto the ice suddenly turned dark and stormy. Wind-driven snow obscured my vision as I tried to follow our guide through the milky mass. Icy pellets struck my helmet with pinging sounds.

After an hour of riding into the opaque void, we parked our snowmobiles and hiked several hundred more feet toward a shadowy formation. Frozen in space and time, a pale yellow ship loomed in front of us as mysterious and impenetrable as the Kremlin during the last decade.

But a different image presented itself inside the vessel. We tramped through warm, inviting rooms that had been restored with wood paneling and brass in the style of the original ship. Built in 1960 and operated as a working icebreaker until 1987 when its width was no longer adequate to open shipping lanes for modern boats, the *Sampo* had been purchased by the city of Kemi. Tourists like my friends and I could experience part of Finland's navigation history first-hand.

Once we were on board, the ship's diesel engines rumbled and we slowly rocked up and down, while inching forward. An icebreaker does not actually plow through the ice, I learned. But rather the ship rides up onto the surface and then crushes the ice with its massive weight.

I stepped outside to get a closer look at this process. While I stood on the deck, I heard the eerie sound of ice smashing combined with the fierce rush of wind. Yet everything seemed to be occurring in slow motion in a strange, lifeless vacuum because the frozen sea did not have any waves. A bizarre Mars-like pattern of cracks shot through the ice just before it split apart into ragged fragments that piled up against each other.

The *Sampo* moved back and forth, clearing an area the size of a Little League baseball diamond. The ship's crew lowered a metal gangway onto the still-frozen perimeter of the makeshift pool.

"Swimming is ready!" Ritva called with delight. "We are first." Those who wished to go into the water – and why wouldn't anyone want to – should come immediately.

After getting dressed in a foam survival suit whose snug-fitting hood left only my eyes, nose and mouth exposed, I walked down the gangway and sat on the edge of the ice. I dangled my legs in the water and a crew member eased me backside in. I immediately drifted away from the "shore" but found that I could steer my movements by paddling with my left arm, right arm, or both. As I bobbed in the pool, I watched my friends slide into the water one after another like slippery seals from rocks.

I paddled back and forth. A fresh layer of snow was collecting on the ice. The wind blew, but I was not cold. Other people speaking different languages were now joining the Arctic pool party. Suddenly I started laughing at the absurdity of this scene as the area became crowded and I bumped into the friendly strangers. I picked up handfuls of ice and tossed the jumbo-sized ice cubes away from me to see them splash and clink in a giant international cocktail.

I couldn't stop laughing, and now Ritva had to coax her once-reluctant swimmers out of the water before the black Arctic nightfall descended. We dressed, ate a salmon dinner on board, and chuckled some more about our strange actions as the ship made its way back to our snowmobile drop-off.

Soon it was time to leave the warmth and safety of the icebreaker, and we suited up in layers, boots and helmets once again. As my friends and I walked into the darkness toward the snow-covered vehicles faintly lit from the ship's ghostly green spotlight, I glanced backward. Silhouetted against the frozen seascape, we looked like a group of aliens who had just landed. We had come a long way, but knew little about our mission in a new world.

I wasn't worried. We had a good team in place.

4. eagle watch

"So you're the birdwatcher," the innkeeper greeted me as I tramped out of the rainy night into the hilltop retreat's cozy Victorian parlor. I had come to the Catskill Mountains in New York State to see and photograph bald eagles, but the chances of seeing any birds, much less our rare national symbol, were looking doubtful.

Despite icy roads, fog and drizzle, my "eagle guide" met me the next morning to answer my questions and point out some of the prime viewing locations.

"We're definitely walking a fine line between promoting this activity and helping people enjoy eagles versus doing something that could potentially harm the resource," said Lori McKean, president of the non-profit Eagle Institute. The self-professed eagle lover and busy mother of three explained the organization's unique program where trained volunteers are stationed at selected points on consecutive weekends. During the winter months when eagles migrate to this area from northern locations in Canada, visitors receive expert assistance in spotting the camera-shy creatures.

As I stood shivering in the "blind" (an unheated wooden shed to conceal human presence) overlooking the frozen landscape at Mongaup Falls, I asked incredulously, "This is where they migrate *to?*"

When their own northern lakes have frozen the eagles seek the open waters of the Delaware River and the various reservoirs in the Catskill Mountain region. Normally human activity would drive the birds away, but in this case the hydro-electric power operations have attracted them by opening up free-flowing channels of water. As an added bonus, the turbines stir up fish and kill them. With free food and a vast, relatively undisturbed habitat, the eagles come here to roost. They cruise the landscape by day and sleep in the trees at night. They don't build nests.

By contrast, the region is also host to a permanent breeding population of bald eagles, but these only number about ten pairs. Indeed, the entire state has less than fifty nesting pairs. However, even this number represents a significant improvement over the 1970s when the population dropped to a single pair due to the combination of DDT and other toxins, the loss of habitat, and man-made hazards such as utility lines and trains. In 1976, New York State launched an aggressive reintroduction program and the population began to rebound.

"I am hearing something," McKean said as we scanned the shoreline of the reservoir for the characteristic white head or any signs of motion in the trees. An eagle is often found when you hear crows, she explained, because the crows harass it and try to force it to drop its catch.

But it was a false alarm, so we moved on. I piled my gear into the car and we drove southeast on Route 97 which parallels the Delaware River along the New York - Pennsylvania border. With low-hanging fog clinging to the hills on the opposite bank of the river, the water tumbled and churned its way swiftly beside us. Chunks of ice raced downstream. Although cars zipped just as quickly down the two-lane highway, the scenic seventy-three-mile stretch is protected from development because it falls under the jurisdiction of the National Park Service.

"Look!" McKean suddenly said, pulling the car onto the road's shoulder. Peering through binoculars, we remained inside our vehicle which served as a blind.

"It's an adult female, about thirteen or fourteen pounds with a full white head."

But still I saw nothing except fuzzy bare-twigged trees in my viewfinder. "No, you're looking in the wrong place," she scolded.

She repositioned my line of sight and magically and majestically the bird popped into view. As if nature were rationing the amount of time I was allowed to peek, the eagle slowly lifted its huge frame into the air and took flight. The bird's motions were neither like the flitting, jumpy takeoff of a song bird nor the flapping, desperate flight of a migrating goose in a V-formation. The eagle simply soared without any apparent effort in maneuvering its seven-foot wingspan. In flight, the white head and white tail feathers became even more prominent.

"I've been doing this seven years and I never get tired of it," McKean emoted.

Buoyed by the prospect that other eagles might be hiding nearby, we drove off once again. I found the exercise to be like a life-size "Where's Waldo" picture or other puzzle you might find in a Sunday newspaper. The little patches of snow that clung to the branches often tricked my eyes into thinking there might be an eagle sitting in the tree, when in fact there was not. Yet McKean could drive the car and readily pick them out with her peripheral vision. She parked the car on the shoulder and this time I got out, positioning the car as a blind between myself and the eagle. McKean watched the bird with binoculars while I set up my tripod.

"She's looking right at you," McKean whispered.

Sure enough, through my camera's lens I saw another female bald eagle surveying the territory that lay beneath the contour of her Romanesque golden beak. She was a beauty and didn't seem to mind posing as long as I kept my distance.

Next we saw a male eagle facing upstream near Staircase Rapids. The male of the species is slightly smaller, McKean explained, and this size difference enables her to make such snap determinations on gender.

"Are there any other clues to finding the eagles?" I wondered. Never mind the sex, it didn't seem as if I would ever be able to spot one on my own.

"Well, you look for other cars pulled off the highway." McKean chuckled. But the comment was only half made in jest. Moments later it proved to be a reliable lead as we chatted alongside the highway with two mild-mannered birdwatchers from neighboring Pennsylvania. The eagles didn't care whether they were in New York or Pennsylvania, and neither did their followers. Like fishermen with binoculars, they were happy to share their stories and commune with others who shared their interest. I was beginning to see how the enthusiasm was infectious.

Indeed, I found myself returning to the area by myself a couple weeks later to get another eagle fix under better weather conditions. The buzz at the Riverview Cafe just over the state border in Lackawaxen, Pennsylvania centered on where the latest eagle sightings had occurred. By lunch time, however, I already had one of my own stories to add into the pot.

Shortly outside Port Jervis, New York, I had pulled into a gravel turnout. I heard crows, looked up and saw two eagles gliding above the tree line on top of the cliff from which the road had been carved. The sun glinting off their white heads and tails, they performed a one-minute ballet against the deep blue sky before disappearing out of sight. A shiver of excitement shot through me. It was a small accomplishment, but in a time when the only place most Americans see our national symbol might be on a slot machine inside a smokey casino, I felt extremely privileged.

"I'm from Brooklyn and have been living here twelve years," McKean had told me at the beginning of our interview. "Eagle watching has become a passion of mine."

Mine too.

5. white dreams

November 8, 1943 *"At night, when I'm in bed, I see myself alone in a dungeon, without Mummy and Daddy. Sometimes I wander by the roadside, or our 'Secret Annexe' is on fire, or they come and take us away at night. I see everything as if it is actually taking place, and this gives me the feeling that it may all happen to me very soon."*
— from *The Diary of a Young Girl* by Anne Frank

At first glance, they didn't look any different than we. Bundled in parkas, hats and blankets, they made their way through the snowy mountains much like us. Back home they drove cars, worked with computers and watched TV. Yet we – an American journalist, a family from Paris and our Canuck guide – were here by choice, on a dogsledding adventure through the Laurentian mountains in French-speaking Quebec Province.

They were making their journey without intent and to unknown destinations. I had watched their televised images like a gruesome dream from which you awake breathlessly and are relieved that it's not real. But as we traveled through our own frozen utopia far away from their vacant faces streaming out of Kosovo, I couldn't stop wondering where dreams ended and reality began.

It certainly seemed real as the weathered, lanky Jean-Francois prepared *les traîneaux à chiens* in the biting morning air at Lac Beauregard. Amid a chorus of thirty-one yelping huskies, he worked quietly and methodically loading supplies, tying lines and double-checking every detail. How the missing middle finger on his left hand resulted, I had neither the language ability nor the courage to ask, but for now it sufficed as testimony to the brutal way of making it in these parts.

We grabbed the wriggling balls of fur and energy, and then pushed noses and paws through openings in the padded harnesses. The barking frenzy intensified when we divided the dogs into five teams and hooked them to the sleds, making sure that the metal anchors were firmly planted in the snow.

As abruptly as the barking began, it stopped when the anchors were lifted and the drivers stepped off the spring-loaded brakes. Initially assigned to passenger status, I felt my sled lurch forward. Soon the motion evened out and the soft whoosh of the wooden runners through the pristine snow was the only sound I heard. With the rhythmic, rocking motion, I hypnotically slipped into dream-like visions whose borders dissolved seamlessly into each other. There were only blue skies and sunshine in this world where cuddly spirits transported us through the vast wilderness and asked for nothing but love in return. Jean-Francois sang a soothing lullaby, and, on cue, frosty evergreens paraded by in step with twenty-eight synchronized paws that kicked up fluffy clouds of light and goodness.

I heard a soft panting and when I looked to my side, I saw that the second team in line was trying to overtake us. Whiskers coated with ice from his frozen breath, the lead dog was like a porcelain statue. Even my friendly pats to his head did not break the intense concentration of the robotic posture.

Reality returned when we stopped for lunch on the trail and parked the sleds. I quickly learned that everyone had a job on this journey. While the dogs simply lay down for a much-deserved rest, we went to work gathering twigs and birch bark. Jean-Francois stamped a square pit into the knee-deep snow and lined it with spruce bows. Within minutes we were warming ourselves beside a crackling fire and talking (as best we could) about our lives.

"France is zee most beautiful country in zee world," proclaimed Jean-Louis, a businessman from Paris. "Unfortunately its people are not."

He must have sensed my astonishment at his bold admission that begged for further explanation. He and his wife, Marie-Laure, a high school math teacher, had traveled to many places in and out of France, showing their children, Veronique (age 16) and Marion (age 13) different ways of life. "My favorite countries are the poorest," he continued. "The people who have the least give the most."

Jean-Louis could not have known that in just a few weeks, Melina, a small village of potato farmers in Macedonia, would offer itself up to Kosovar refugees. The residents would give what little they had to those even less fortunate than they. Their own children's schools would become shelters as desks were turned into beds. Their own food would feed others.

We sipped hot tea poured from thermal bottles and devoured pork chops grilled over the fire. Indeed, all the meals we were to eat were meat-based and high-fat, but tasted good outdoors and provided the energy needed to keep us going in the extreme cold.

Like Jean-Francois snuffing out the final wafting aroma of balsam from the dying coals, any lingering illusory state of consciousness was also abruptly erased later that afternoon. With Veronique at the helm this time, once again I had been riding as a passenger, lulled into the crystal netherworld between sky and earth.

The sun was lower on the horizon and I was chilled. The sled was gaining momentum as the dogs began to race full speed down hill. The dogs turned left, the sled tipped over on the right, and I fell out. I landed on top of the anchor whose two points hit squarely on each thigh. The dogs kept running, however, dragging me several more feet. My clothes were ripped and my legs cut and bruised, but the wounds were not severe. Tugging and nipping at each other, the dogs ended in a jumble of tangled lines.

Lest the canine discord have been an example of finely tuned teamwork gone awry, our newly bonded human team set to work immediately upon arrival at Camp Revelstone – a simple building with bunk beds and a wood-burning stove. Jean-Francois built a fire, Marie-Laure sewed my torn clothing, and we fed the dogs. We dipped pots into an unfrozen stream to obtain water for drinking, cooking and washing. Was I dreaming when Jean-Louis began to sing French opera and everyone joined in? Here were teenagers who didn't think their father's boisterous antics were the least bit corny. Here were people who truly enjoyed being together as a family for this special time far away from their home.

As the famished kids scrambled for toast made by putting bread slices onto the scorching stove top and then flipping them onto the table, the adults joined in the game. The similarities to tent camps in Albania, Montenegro and Macedonia, where refuges grabbed for loaves of bread tossed out of relief vehicles, were striking; the differences haunting. Only the person's ethnicity caused him or her to fall into one group or the other.

The next day I was sufficiently knowledgeable about dogsledding to drive a team myself. I tried memorizing the dogs' names as I hitched them in the precise positions that Jean-Francois had pre-defined. My lead dog, Anouk, obediently took off when I chortled "hip," the command for "go." The other six dogs, arranged two by two, simultaneously began pulling, and we slid out onto frozen Lake Revelstone. Soon I sensed that the dogs accepted me so that in due time we were able to establish a comfortable, steady pace. They didn't know or care that I was different and that I didn't coo in French. We were simply a unit.

The teenage girls, of course, knew I was culturally different than them, but we enjoyed and teased about our diversity. I practiced my French and they their English.

"David is fun," Marion proudly said in perfect English, surprising and delighting her parents one day.

"David is funny," the older sister, Veronique said, enjoying the play on words and seeing my mock agitation. She was soon begging me to reveal the latest plot developments of the sitcom *Friends'* episodes which are popular in France but air considerably later than in the U.S.

Was our cross-cultural comraderie out of the ordinary, I wondered. Were we a minority living in a dream world insulated from inherently more sinister forces?

Standing with one foot on each runner, I looked just beyond my canine reality filter to the harsh environment beyond. Crossing the lake were tracks of wolves who had cruised the camp the previous night in search of a kill. Further into the woods, Jean-Francois pointed out lynx tracks which dead ended at various trees where the big cats ambushed their bird prey. In this universe, the omnipresent predators seemed inevitable.

Indeed, that was how the early French settlers colonized this region where winter's icy grip hangs on forever. Out of necessity, they had to become the predators, shooting and trapping otters, beavers, sables, minks and martens. It was the law of survival.

But for now, I reveled in the purity of the white dream, merely shifting my weight left and right, or commanding "ha" and "gee" to control my destiny. Real life should be that simple.

The remainder of my journey through the wilderness passed pleasantly and uneventfully, but I never quite felt I left the fantasy, even after I said *au revoir* to the dogs and to my French friends. I still recalled all these transitory images as I drove out of the area and stopped to spend a day of skiing at Mont Tremblant, a glitzy resort fashioned after the streets of New Orleans' French Quarter.

I listened to the car radio playing a local call-in talk show whose angry guests spewed inflammatory rhetoric directed at one class of citizen or another in the province. It was difficult to listen to the hatred in the voices. Presumably Milosevic gained power the same way by inflaming ethnic passions. With the flick of my wrist, I turned it off. Ah well, I had one more day to enjoy this winter wonderland.

At the ski rental shop, the young clerk, seeing that I was American, decided I needed a thorough Canadian history lesson before being turned loose. "... and so Quebec is a province and culture just waiting to be discovered," he finally concluded. "The strife you hear about is all political. The people don't care about any of that."

I prayed I wasn't still dreaming.

spring

6. the brink

It was the season that wasn't a season. Winter was over, and the ice was gone from the mountain lakes of upstate New York's Adirondacks. Spring hadn't arrived yet. But as my canoe sliced its way into the dormant landscape, I knew that we were on the edge.

The black flies that emerged from the darkly mirrored water and skittered above the surface belied the cool, early May air as my guide Brian took the lead while his assistant, Cindy, and I followed.

Everywhere we turned, the next generation beckoned. Apparently lifeless forms called out for attention. Standing like exclamation points against the bare-twigged trees lining the shore, white birches punctuated the expressionless background. "Wake up, everybody!" they cried. "Look at us!" Following their call to action, we splashed our way through Second Stony Creek Pond into Stony Creek itself.

We floated over a collapsed beaver dam, the two- to three-inch logs still crisscrossed in acknowledgment of its former architectural eminence. Further downstream, freshly gnawed wood initiated the process anew in the beavers' perpetual attempts to raise the water level and create pools of life-sustaining water.

Each turn seemed to suggest something beyond the present state. We rounded a bend, and I saw the sandy bottom's grassy tentacles waving in the gently flowing stream and trying to catch enough light that would soon turn them green. "This way!" they coaxed, while bottom-feeding suckers disobediently darted upstream in their annual spawning ritual.

We drifted past marshy flats where bushy red-stemmed clumps of vegetation sheltered potential prey from the snare of a hawk silently circling overhead. I heard only the steady, soothing drip of water as it rolled off my paddle and hit the creek. But further downstream, the quicker-paced rat-a-tat-tat tempo of a woodpecker clinging to the side of a limbless tree trunk caught my attention. "Faster!" it cried. "Faster!"

Perfecting our turning technique, we zigged and zagged through the myriad of switchbacks that the creek took to its juncture with the Raquette River. In a raspy, squirrel-like chatter, the bluish gray Kingfisher bird with its punk rock hair-do played cat and mouse with us. "Here I am," it teased, and flew further away. Around each new bend of our private information superhighway lay a sensory signpost that pointed us toward the future.

*   *   *

The following morning the haunting yodel of the loons lured us back into the aquatic theater. "Easy there, big guys," the loons whimpered as they steered away from the floating yellow monsters and dove under the water of Little Clear Pond, resurfacing a suspense-filled minute later.

Following the route of the "Seven Carries," we paddled to the opposite shore and hauled the canoes overland to the next waterway. We navigated through the narrow channel of a bog where carnivorous pitcher plants sat in open-mouthed anticipation for a taste of the season's first insects. "Just you wait!" they yawned.

We paddled across Saint Regis Pond rimmed with mountains where the deciduous trees would soon be roughhousing in the wind with their evergreen siblings.

"Grace and I were married on this lake last year." Brian pointed toward a small island as the first spring peepers squeaked their approval from the sidelines. They would be undergoing their own mating ritual on these same waters.

We cruised across the diminutive Green Pond whose algae population was busy dressing it with its namesake color. An osprey soared over Little Long Pond, guarding its bulky nest perched sixty feet above us in the top of a tree where the next generation would learn to take flight.

Everywhere I turned it seemed that the "dormant" facade was on the brink. Like much of human experience, the preparation itself magnified the act. Nature awaited something beyond its current state. It anticipated the renewal of spring and the abundance of summer in the mountains. We paddled on.

At Bear Pond we circled the swimming rock where school-weary adolescents within the months ahead would be diving from its surface into the refreshing depths below. I tip-toed along a log as we launched into Bog Pond. At Upper Saint Regis Lake, Cindy picked up a few pine cones for her craft projects. They were still closed and had not yet dispersed their seeds. She would dry them on the fireplace until they popped open.

"The color is more intense," she explained, "when you gather them just before they're ready to open."

Although I had never made pine cone wreaths, I agreed.

7. the kalmiopsis chronicles

The sea was dark and moody and so was the lighthouse keeper. In the blinding lantern room of Cape Blanco lighthouse on Oregon's southern coast, I could sense that the silhouetted figure was eyeing me suspiciously.

"Don't touch that!" he suddenly barked as I extended my finger toward the prisms of the rotating octagonal lens that cast an intermittent beacon onto the churning waters. He was playing a role, slipping in and out of character as James Langlois, the nineteenth century civil servant who spent each day of his thirty-six-year tenure carrying oil up the winding stairway, trimming the wick and polishing the lens. The slightest departure from the routine could have sent a ship crashing into the dangerous reefs below. His life had a consistency that provided security to passing ships, and I suspected, to himself as well.

But tonight, the actor would leave the now-electrified light unattended, go home, and get on with more complex twentieth century decisions. And when the lighthouse beam faded into morning, I would explore the area that it had guarded over the past two centuries.

Indeed, with 7/8 of Oregon coast as public land, by outward appearances the area appeared steady and unchanging. However, I learned that most of the coastline is sinking into the ocean while Cape Blanco is rising at the rate of one inch per year – quite rapid in geological terms and volatile enough to set off a number of small tremors. But of late the major shockwaves have been in the economic climate of the region. As the area tries to rebound from the decline of the timber industry by moving toward a tourism-based economy, it struggles to preserve the natural beauty of the landscape that attracts people to the coast.

Soon I found myself bouncing along the gravel roads of a 900-acre ranch while my "vehicle safari" leader leaned out her window.

"Hello babies! Here babies!" she cooed. Lidia had spotted the newborn offspring of the resident elk herd that grazed on the land. I looked beyond the idyllic pasture to see mountainsides sporting a checkerboard pattern of clear-cut, replanted and old-growth forests.

"I never thought I'd take up ranching at this point in my life," she said in a Polish accent that had lingered since her arrival in the U.S. as a political refugee at age nineteen almost thirty years ago.

"How did you and Stephen find your way to Oregon?" I wondered. Her curly, blonde hair was pulled back in a sort of updated Janis Joplin look. The faded jeans and matching denim vest somehow looked more stylish and functional than rebellious. But the ensuing story of fate and circumstance fell into place, tumbling out more haphazardly than the white waters of the Rogue River that rushed through the valley below.

They were the quintessential New Age couple. She had arrived in America with little more than pocket change when she met Stephen, a handsome Bostonian personifying the idealism of the sixties. They spent a year together, but decided they needed to move on and go their separate ways. Colorado sounded good, and could she hitch a ride as long as they were both headed west?

Like the plot from a "road flick," by the time they hit the Rockies, they were more deeply in love than they had realized. Their youthful naivete took them to an artsy enclave in the mountains of northern New Mexico where they tried to earn a living making candles. Unbeknownst to them, they had set up shop in the same town as a major candle manufacturer.

A series of moves and smart real estate deals had brought better fortune in the years ahead. They survived the stress of raising two children and were living a comfortable life. But on a visit to this little-known part of the Oregon coast, the lifetime Sierra Club members fell in love with the land. Winter Springs Ranch was too much of a bargain to pass up. In their forties, when most people have settled into the places and patterns that define their lives, they packed their white water rafts and meditation books once again.

Lidia shifted the vehicle into four-wheel drive and we climbed to the top of a hill. She lovingly identified each of the towering Douglas firs, redwoods, cedars and Ponderosa pines that we passed, scoffing at the lucrative sums logging companies had offered for the trees.

"We have thousands of trees, but it's hard to cut even one," she confessed. In fact, since acquiring the ranch in 1988, she had already planted 210,000 more trees in an attempt to reverse some of the environmental damage that cattle farming had caused in earlier times.

That evening, as my hosts and I sipped wine in the brand new guest house, I sat at the granite counter and watched the fog hanging on the lush greens of the hilltops surrounding us. Gone were the cattle, scorned were the timber interests. I tried to imagine visitors mountain biking through the forests, taking gourmet cooking lessons, or attending Tai Chi workshops...

Throughout my visit I learned that Oregon safeguards its treasures carefully. The land yields a gem only to the few it has deemed fortunate or those who have worked hard enough. From the shadows of a misty drive along the coastal highway, a rainbow appears and teases me to climb among the rocks. Or I dip my feet in a stream's teal-colored pool, but only after hiking through a canyon in ninety-degree heat.

Some places are even so special that residents guard their whereabouts from the outside world. But they, too, are ambivalent. On the one hand, they're proud of what Oregon has to offer and want to share it with respectful, appreciative visitors. On the other hand, they don't want an influx of people to ruin the solitude of these unique spots.

My friend Bob, himself a recent transplant to Oregon, agreed to take me to one of these places if I promised not to write about it.

"But I'm a journalist," I protested. "That's my job."

So we compromised. We'd hike. I'd write. But I wouldn't pinpoint the location, and if readers wanted to come with a local guide, that would be OK.

A cold front had moved in off the ocean, clearing the sky and causing a stiff northwesterly wind. We hiked through pine forests, rhododendron patches and sandy dunes until we reached land's end. The scene lying in front of me was so captivating that I spent the next hour mesmerized.

A stream zigzagged through the marshy flat onto sandstone where it dropped two hundred feet to the sea below me. The gusty wind forced the waterfall to flow up and back into the air over the point of land where the water droplets sparkled in the sunlight.

RARE SPECIES

Like the gold rush of 1853 that brought prospectors to the coast and smiled on the chosen, Oregon revealed one of its treasures and rewarded Baldassare Mineo, the grandson of Italian immigrants. Raised in southern California, he earned his college degree majoring in architecture. His love of plants, however, eventually brought him to Oregon where he established a successful nursery business specializing in rare plants.

As I walked past the breathtaking rock gardens, ponds and displays, he told me about one of the mainstays of the nursery, a tiny evergreen with the botanical name *Kalmiopsis*. Indigenous to the Siskiyou mountain range in southern Oregon, *Kalmiopsis* is a prehistoric species that survived nowhere else. No more than a few inches tall and topped with delicate pink flowers, the plant is a precursor to our popular modern-day azaleas and rhododendrons. Other unique plants are found only in the Siskiyous. I wanted to know why this area was such a treasure trove of botanical species.

"This is the southernmost range of some arctic plants," he explained, pulling a weed from the manicured paths that we walked along, "and the northernmost range of some California plants."

"The east-west orientation of the mountains acted as a barrier to migration. Some species were protected here because they were not subjected to the volcanic activity of the surrounding ranges." His mane of black hair and Italian-Greek features gave him a look as exotic as the plants underfoot. He was different, a survivor taking hold in an isolated niche.

Wherever I turned, there were survivors, people who were finding their place in the splendor and unique beauty of the Oregon coast. On a drizzly, foggy morning I hiked on the Redwood Nature Trail and segments of the Oregon Coast Trail.

Walking up to a redwood twelve feet in diameter, my guide Mark stretched his arms around it in a playful hug.

"Why would anyone want to cut one?" he lamented. "People should come up and pet 'em, not put a chain saw to 'em."

Mark grew up in an era when young men went to work for logging companies after they graduated from high school. But at eighteen he saw the handwriting on the wall. The timber industry had been in steady decline. Gold Beach, once a bustling mill town, now had no lumber mills. Most of the old-growth forests of Douglas fir had been logged out. Only 3-6 percent of the original redwood stands still remained. So he joined the merchant marines. Of the last twenty years, seventeen had been spent at sea.

But now he was back, embarking on a new phase in life, and looking at his home with a freshness that only time and distance could provide. We walked, we hopped, we dodged, we stooped to examine every tree and leaf in the coastal rain forest. We were on a schedule.

"Low tide is at 11:45 this morning." Mark glanced at his watch. "We're doing good. Look at the size of that trillium there. It's a honker."

He wanted to get down to the beach to show me an isolated cove situated between headlands – those points of land comprised of steep cliffs jutting into the sea. Secret Beach was accessible only during low tide when you could safely walk around the base of the northern headland.

So off we trudged past Oregon big leaf maples, red alders and tan oaks, brushing against witch's hair and stepping over banana slugs. I chewed the twisted root of a licorice fern and snacked on juicy salmonberries that hung in golden-orange clusters. Uh oh, now we *were* running late.

We took a shortcut off the trail and scampered down a steep fern-covered bank until we landed on the sandy flats. Waves lapped onto the shore. Looming in front of me in the ocean was a "sea stack," an upright rocky island that had been severed from the mainland by eons of wave action. Through my binoculars I watched the Pacific harbor seals lolling on some rocks at the base of the sea stack.

I could also see starfish clinging in rows to the sides of the rocks where the departing tide had left them exposed to the air. The sky grew brighter and the sun broke out, lifting the fog in swirling patterns and creating an iridescent blue sheen on the sea. We walked along the shore and poked our noses into a spooky cave that had been hollowed out of one cliff.

At the headland, waves rolled against the rocky, irregular surfaces, and splashed up against the cliff. Just around the corner lay Secret Beach, but there was no direct path into the cove. I looked at Mark.

"Tides vary. Some low tides are lower than others." He looked apologetic.

I knew his look meant that the water was as low as it was going to get. To go into the cove we would need to wade through water on slippery rocks, and if we stayed too long we could be trapped by the rising tide.

"I'm game," I said.

Without dawdling we climbed onto the barnacle- and mussel-encrusted rocks, the icy salt water flowing over my sneakers and ankles. Each time the water retreated, I gingerly stepped to the next foothold and handhold, hoping to make the move before another wave splashed back in. But during one cycle I was caught mid-wave and water spurted over my knees up to my waist.

Soon we made it off the rocks and were back on level ground. I was able to stand upright and inspect some of the rocks on the dry side of the cliff. At eye level there was a ledge with a scooped-out square bowl the size of a microwave oven. The forces of nature had created a mini-aquarium and populated it with some seaweed, a single starfish and a turquoise sea anemone. The makeshift community looked established and natural but would probably be ripped loose and replaced by the next tide.

We had only a few minutes to explore. Feet squishing inside my sneakers, I walked over the pristine sand to the center of the cove and looked at the sea straight ahead framed by cliffs rising on each side. There were no roads, no paths, no clear entrance or exit points. This scene existed only at this moment. How had we arrived here? Maybe like the sea creatures clinging to the rocks it was a little by design, mostly by happenstance. We wouldn't be here long.

A large wave rolled in and crashed against the cliff. We had to get going, as the foamy surf was already starting to move back in and fill our little chunk of space and time.

"Ready, guy?" Mark called.

"Where are we going next?" I asked just as another wave crashed. He hadn't heard me.

But could I really have expected an answer? After all, this was the sea, the end of the road, where reality leads to wishing, wishes lead to dreaming, and dreams and opportunities come and go as quickly as the passing tides.

8. a lost world

Standing on the site of a former mahogany logging camp in Central America, I discovered a new planet.

The cloudless night sky over Belize was crisp in the center, while murky edges crept in where the horizon met the rainforest. My astronomer-host at the remote jungle lodge checked her notes, programmed the coordinates and tapped some commands into the motorized refracting telescope which slowly rotated on its base and zoomed into focus. Hiding as infinitesimal specks among the billions of other twinkly points spread across light-years of space and time, we located globular clusters, nebulae and distant galaxies.

I thought it strange to be using such hi-tech equipment in a third-world nation that didn't even have reliable electricity or phone service. But the astronomer's unusual mix of right- and left-brain activity perplexed me even further. Carolyn Carr was an accomplished artist. I had just strolled through her studio filled with romanticized paintings of jaguars, birds and Mayan Indians.

"For me, I think it's the certainty," she said, directing my line of sight to a glowing hat-shaped formation appropriately nicknamed the "sombrero galaxy." "I can always look up and see the stars in exactly the same position."

That night I could have stayed up till dawn watching the infinite patterns of light and listening to the raucous buzz of cicadas, but I had another active day planned for tomorrow. I soon retired to the four-poster bed inside my thatched-roof cabana and pulled down the mosquito netting. After the generator shut down for the night and the overhead fan stopped its hypnotic whirl, the smell of smoke from distant slash-and-burn operations crept into the room. I lay there a while thinking about what I had just seen during my week-long adventure into the Cayo district in the interior of Belize.

I saw great cities. But there were no theaters, restaurants or shops. There weren't even any residents. I had jounced over rutty limestone roads and crossed muddy rivers with hand-cranked wooden ferries to arrive at sites where these metropolises once ruled over the surrounding jungles in the Yucatan peninsula.

At Xunantunich (pronounced Shoo-NAN-Tune-Itch) which was flourishing in the year A.D. 600 – and abandoned by A.D. 1000 – I climbed to the top of the 130-foot tall Mayan pyramid. Legend has it that a maiden appeared here one night and dissolved into the stone. Folklore notwithstanding, I was on a point that archaeologists now believed to be an observatory from which priests surveyed the heavens and made declarations to farmers on when and what to plant. Known as an astronomical frieze, the outside walls of the temple were comprised of bigger-than-life limestone carvings of the sun god, moon god and rain god, and left no doubt that such deities dominated every aspect of Mayan society.

At Caracol, whose population was estimated to be as high as 500,000 residents, my Belizean guide Mr. Buckley paused at a fiberglass replica of a stele. The upright monoliths were erected as markers to signify the conquest of one city-state over another. The hieroglyphic-like scenes always had one thing in common: the conquering leader looked to the right while the defeated leader faced left.

"What happened to the original stele?" I wondered.

"It's in Britain," Mr. Buckley said coolly. But I could tell the seething anger had an even more disturbing root cause than the reckless looting of important archaeological treasures during the days when Belize was a British colony.

Having served sixteen years in the British army, Mr. Buckley, a loyal British subject himself, was guiding an Englishman around the Caracol site in 1970. He told his fellow countryman the location of the stele. Two weeks later a helicopter appeared above the rainforest canopy and lifted the rock away.

"If only I had known, I wouldn't have shown him," Mr. Buckley said. "If only I had known."

Today official Belize petitions continue to the governments of England, Canada and other nations where the Mayan artifacts are located, but the requests are always turned down with a "finders-keepers" justification.

While the causes of the twentieth-century cultural erosion are easily identified, the agents responsible for that occurring in prior centuries are not as clear cut. Wandering among the open courtyards and piles of rubble, I slathered on sunscreen and became an amateur archaeologist for a few hours. I climbed steep steps and poked into pitch-black cubbyholes. Letting my imagination run wild, I tried to imagine what forces in society built jail cells and throne rooms, sacrificed children and celebrated marriages.

It seems everyone has his own theory on the collapse of Mayan civilization. Basing his ideas on the pre-excavation condition of these cities, Mr. Buckley feels that the Mayans evacuated in a planned, orderly fashion.

"These rocks didn't just climb up there," he said, pointing to the debris that covered the temples – a contrast to the central plaza's absence of such material. "Maybe the Mayans covered the structures as we might board up a house that we know is going to be empty for a long time."

At the El Pilar site, which spans a tract on both sides of the Guatemala-Belize border, I suggested this theory to Dr.

Annabel Ford, a research archaeologist at the MesoAmerican Research Center of the University of California. The idea was met with skepticism.

"You're simply seeing the result of a thousand years of abandonment," she said. "Why the Mayans came and why they left is no mystery. This was an agrarian society – ninety-five percent were farmers. They came because there was food. They left when it ran out." End of discussion.

Why the food would run out and where the Mayans would go was not as obvious to me. Currently, rainforest was being cleared for agriculture *because* the land was fertile and the climate was perfect for crops. And people of Mayan descent still comprised a significant part of the ethnic mixture known as the "Belize boiler." During my stay, drivers, guides and scientists alike often told me about the knowledge and cultural values a Mayan parent or grandparent imparted. Every native Belizean I met knew how to cure a headache, lower a fever or stop diarrhea by simply chewing on a leaf or swallowing a seed he or she had collected from the forest.

As I rode horseback through villages and jungle terrain, following the lead horse with my barefoot, machete-wielding guide hacking at bark, vines and roots, I was struck by the contrast between the sparseness of Belizean lives and the richness of their environment. Standing outside ramshackle houses, naked toddlers watched the curious gringo laden with expensive photographic equipment pass by. Just beyond their doorways lay potential cures for cancer, AIDS and other devastating diseases. The discovery of one blockbuster drug could lift the entire nation out of third-world status overnight and have far-reaching impacts in other parts of the world. Yet, in order to survive in the present, the very resource that held that future was being destroyed at an alarming rate.

There is a Mayan saying which states that for every problem in nature, there is a solution to be found in nature. I spoke with one resident – an expatriate American – who is working to preserve both that body of knowledge and the plant species themselves before they disappear altogether.

Dr. Rosita Arvigo came to Belize in 1983 for what she terms "medical freedom" – the ability to practice medicine outside the existing conventions of the United States medical establishment. She employs traditional Mayan treatments which include herbs found in the rainforest. Having lived in Central America and studied herbalism for a number of years, she gained further expertise when she became an apprentice to Don Eligio Panti, an elderly Mayan shaman (doctor-priest). Panti passed away at age 103 in 1996, but not before Dr. Arvigo had documented his vast repertoire of cures.

I sipped chilled mint tea under the shade of a little pavilion at her home while listening to success stories of past cases. Most of the patients had come from the U.S. where they were dissatisfied with the care they were receiving. Dr. Arvigo has had particular success with an infertility treatment developed from an ancient Mayan massage technique. Combined with herbal remedies to cleanse the uterus, the Mayo-Uterine massage, she claimed, had resulted in a welcome pregnancy in one woman who had tried for fifteen years to become pregnant.

Looking very earthy herself, Dr. Arvigo gave me a crash lesson in tropical botany and invited me to stroll on the Medicine Trail, a secluded footpath with the various curative plants growing in their natural habitat. Rustic labels and a carry-along, time-worn guidebook identified the various species.

As if being transported through a hushed, darkened time tunnel, I slowly walked down the roughhewn trail, pinpointing individual plants intertwined in the lush tangle of tropical vegetation above, below, and on each side of me. Roots and vines hung seemingly in mid-air.

It was not hard to see how the rich diversity of botanical species could live in synchronicity – synthesizing, harboring and releasing the myriads of compounds that each needed to flourish. How could I assume that the human species, which had evolved on this same planet, was not part of this intricate web? Were we so technologically advanced that we had forgotten what the Mayan shamans knew and practiced for centuries? How many millions of as-yet-undiscovered species and compounds lay waiting in these hidden recesses of the earth?

These were concerns that Dr. Arvigo was acutely aware of. The Medicine Trail is actually part of a 6,000-acre reserve. Not only does the rainforest live and breathe in relative safety here, but it has become an environmental orphanage to threatened botanical species from other parts of Belize. When tracts of land are about to be opened for agriculture or development, the newly uncovered species from the land are collected and transplanted here.

Preservation is only one part of Dr. Arvigo's mission, however. In collaboration with the New York Botanical Garden, she is participating in the long-term Belize Ethnobotany Project whose primary goal is to test the plants' effectiveness in fighting cancer and AIDS. Plant samples are shipped back to the U.S. for testing. The project is partially funded by the U.S. Agency for International Development, an arm of the U.S. State Department. Belize has a contract that stipulates should a drug be developed from one of these plants, the nation obtains a share of the profits. The traditional healers may then petition the Belize government for compensation.

Although it appears that everyone benefits from this arrangement, the system is not well-oiled or even tested, and the consensus of opinion is far from unanimous. Some of Don

Eligio Panti's children and grandchildren think that he was working with the devil. Many shamans still have not been identified and their cures documented. Like the cities of their ancestors, might their knowledge slip into the clutches of the jungle, to surface centuries later or possibly never again?

During the remainder of my trip through the Cayo district, I paddled down rivers, waded beneath pristine waterfalls, watched shimmering blue morpho butterflies flutter in the breeze, and listened to armadillos rustle in the crackly fallen leaves of the dry season. I released endangered green iguanas hatched and raised under protective custody and crawled through caves exploring what the Mayans believed to be secret entrances to the underworld.

But now I lay in the motionless air amid the swirl of memories, separated from reality by only the protective veil of the mosquito netting. I had a hard time falling asleep so I wandered outside to see how the jungle did it. The rhythmic progression of cycles, whether daily or seasonal, seemed pre-defined and predictable, unlike our own species which had so many options and worries. As humans, we had the capacity to love, to hate; to build, to destroy; to ail, to heal. The choices seemed entirely ours. I looked up to the heavens once more before going inside, but I didn't need a telescope this time because the planet I had just discovered was not in the sky above me. It was under my feet.

9. fast, dangerous and wet?

"I don't know what a windjammer is," my friend chirped before driving off with my car and leaving me to board the local ferry that would shuttle me across mid-coast Maine's Penobscot Bay, "but it sounds fast, dangerous and wet."

"I hope so," I said.

The ferry's engine rumbled, and along with a handful of walk-on passengers and a half-dozen cars, pickups and delivery vehicles making their morning commute to Islesboro Island, I slipped almost as cluelessly into the pea-soup fog. I did know that windjammers were large sailboats originally built to transport freight along the New England coast. The ships carried items such as fish and lumber from Maine to the bustling harbors of Boston and New York.

Fifteen minutes later, I stepped off the vibrating metal and strolled around the deserted wooden docks. In the distance I saw the double-masted schooner *Lewis R. French* drifting slowly through the mist. Why wasn't it speeding over to get me? Why wasn't it kicking up any waves? Who were those people casually standing around? And why weren't they wearing bright yellow rain slickers?

"Hi, my name is 'Sinker.'" As if I had stepped through a curtain of fog into a *Gilligan's Island* rerun, the slight frame appeared from nowhere and led me down a set of wooden stairs to the water. I could imagine only one way he would have earned that name. Of course this trip will be fast, dangerous and wet, I concluded. I climbed into a tiny boat with an outboard motor that gurgled in unison with Sinker's voice.

"This is a yawl boat," he explained. "It tows the ship when needed. Other than the wind, there's no other propulsion on a schooner."

"Speaking of wind, is there enough of it?" I asked.

"It's a little light, but it'll be OK."

We sputtered away from the dock into open waters and soon two full sails loomed in front of me. I climbed from the yawl up a short ladder onto the varnished pine deck of the sixty-five-foot schooner. In mocking anticipation of more interesting weather, my mind hummed the lines from the *Gilligan's Island* theme: "the weather started getting rough… the tiny ship was tossed…"

Nevertheless, I found a unique solace in watching the mist swirl gently on the water and rise until it evaporated in the brightening sky. The rolling hills of the coastline emerged and grew greener by the passing minute. Islands sauntered by.

"Do we need to trim the jib and the foresail?" asked Greg, a computer analyst from California who'd been a windjammer passenger so often that the owner had let him take the wheel.

"Nah. They look good," Skipper Dan replied.

Gentle puffs of wind filled the sails maneuvered into precisely the right positions by an impressively engineered system of ropes and wooden pulleys strung from the eighty-two-foot high Douglas fir masts. At the top of the masts, flags fluttered in the breeze. The ship's course that I had earlier deemed as boring and meandering now appeared steady and unwavering along the coast.

We passed a school of porpoises that broke through the water surface for a breath of the cool, salty air and then disappeared. Meanwhile, the cook surfaced from the ship's galley and rang the polished brass bell calling us to a breakfast of bacon, scrambled eggs, potatoes, macaroni and melon. Between sips of coffee, we rested our filled mugs on gleaming wood surfaces without spilling so much as a drop, and drank in the ever-changing panorama of serendipitous coves sprinkled with white clapboard buildings. Life was good.

Perched on top of a cabin, I listened to the small waves lapping at the sides of the ship as we glided past an assortment of bobbers marking the locations of lobster traps in the bay. The bobbers within each grouping had their own distinct color and pattern to identify their ownership.

The sun poked out and reflected off the shiny surfaces of the mariner's instrument panel. Behind one circle of glass, a quivering needle hovered at 2.9 knots – barely a brisk walk.

Skipper Dan noticed my fascination with the instruments. "You should've been with us yesterday. We were really cruisin'," he said. "We had twenty-knot winds."

But the funny thing was, that, by now, I didn't mind. I spent the rest of the morning without going fast, encountering danger or getting wet – and liked it. As the sails were lowered and we skated gracefully into Camden harbor, the peaceful feeling lingered. Maybe cluelessness wasn't such a bad thing after all. For a while, it felt good to be clueless, to lie back and enjoy smooth sailing while it lasted.

10. a democracy timeline

The melodic chanting of Buddhist monks drifts through the still atmosphere. I float just as idly down the silty water of the Ayeyarwady River through the mysterious land once known as Burma, and now called the Union of Myanmar. White-washed and gold-plated temples glistening in the tropical sun cover the distant hills.

I cannot distinguish past, present and future. On the satellite-fed television stations beamed down to my ship cabin, I follow the events on the other side of the globe.

March 7, 2000 (Super Tuesday) This is the high-stakes day on which candidates for the United States presidency hope to win enough votes that will assure their party's nomination. Large numbers of votes in many key states are up for grabs today.

Texas Governor George W. Bush trounces his Republican rival, Arizona Senator John McCain, winning California, New York and five other primaries. McCain, however, sweeps five New England states, pocketing 102 delegates. In the Democratic party primaries, Vice President Al Gore wins every state over Bill Bradley.

I look up from the CNN broadcast to see small tent camps of itinerant fishing families on sandy banks where the water has receded during the dry season in the central plains. On the river itself, an occasional floating Huck Finn style platform of bamboo and wood logs drifts by. The raft itself is the cargo, making its four-week journey to the river delta where it will be dismantled and sold. From a thatched hut perched on top, family members cheerfully wave back. Less than fifteen percent of Myanmar's population has electricity, much less television.

March 6, 2000 Thus far the lackluster political campaigns have not held much interest for me. As Will Rogers once said, "I don't belong to any organized political party. I'm a Democrat." The economy is good. Americans are traveling overseas in record numbers. There are no major domestic issues.

But the campaign of a maverick senator has caught the nation's attention and energized the political process. Speaking at a rally in Santa Clara, California, John McCain addresses the diverse crowd of Republicans, independents, Democrats, libertarians and vegetarians. "We hope to involve young people in democracy again," he says.

(Earlier that day) Squares of bright green rice paddies among shiny irrigation channels come into focus as my flight descends into Myanmar's capital city, Yangon. We walk across the tarmac to the terminal building flanked with gold columns and ornate carvings.

On the other side of immigration, our bronze-skinned guide, Khan Yang Hu (name changed) greets us wearing the traditional *longyi*, a loose-fitting cylindrical plaid garment longer than a kilt and knotted in the center to hold it around the waist. Calloused feet in stiff sandals lead us away.

During our stay in Myanmar, we can take pictures of beautiful buildings and people. But we should not take pictures of soldiers or military trucks. "It will be a big problem for you and for me," Khan says.

March 5, 2000, Chiang Mai, northern Thailand Unofficial results filter in from Thailand's first-ever senate election. Previously, the senators were government appointees. An article in the *Bangkok Post* estimates that the makeup of the 200-seat senate would consist of about seventy percent entrenched ex-politicians, their relatives and other influential people. But results show that only forty-eight percent represent the old guard. Social-minded candidates like former teacher Mrs. Prateep Ungsongham Hata who helped slum areas acquire schools were elected in overwhelming numbers.

We drive along teak-lined boulevards and wind into the hills. High above the valleys at 3,000 feet we visit the temple Doi Suthep whose *stupa* (large solid steeple) reportedly houses remains of Buddha. The reason Thailand's King built the temple at this particular location, the legend goes, is that the royal elephant carrying the remains ran away and stood ground on this site.

Today, the once-revered beasts play harmonicas, kick balls and roll over for tourists. At the Maesa Elephant Camp, I watch giggly women climb upon their trunks while trainers firmly hold tender ear tissue wrapped around a hook.

March 4, 2000 My steward pokes his head into the cozy lacquered-teak cabin as the train clickety clacks into the sunrise.

"Would you be for more coffee, sir?" he asks, silver tray in hand. Little farms with citrus groves, banana patches and vegetable plots dot the parched, viney jungle passing outside my window. A sleepy little boy in pajamas standing barefoot at the end of his dusty road watches the green and yellow cars snake past him.

I'm en route to northern Thailand through the main valley that stretches between Bangkok and Chiang Mai. Meanwhile across the country, Thais are flocking to the polls in record numbers.

"You have a beautiful brain line," the psychic tells me as I sit with palms upturned in the library car. "But your money line is short." Astrology and prophecy have long played a role throughout southeast Asia from naming children to building temples. Many important political decisions are made only after consulting with psychics. I think about the uproar over Nancy Reagan's secret astrology readings in the White House in the 1980s.

March 3, 2000 Purple orchids hang from trees along a Bangkok street as we creep through the noisy sea of vehicles on our way to the Grand Palace. Buses, cars, motorcycles and three-wheeled taxis known as *tuk-tuks* all compete for space. Vendors walk among the standing traffic to sell jasmine garlands which can be offered to Buddha. To each side of me, political posters for the upcoming senate election are hung in store windows, strung across bank buildings, and pasted on lamp posts. Every candidate is identified with a number. Number 104 is a middle-aged woman who reminds you of the high school teacher who could silence a roomful of rowdy adolescents with just a glare. She is dressed in a military uniform. Perhaps to soften the image she is trying to convey to Thai voters in the "land of smiles," the candidate's portrait is positioned inside a big, pink heart.

We wander among the serene grounds of a monastery, visit an island where women make a traditional candy from duck egg yolks, and go to a pottery factory where skinny boys with snaky tattoos spin clay to the beat of Thai rock playing from a boom box. At the end of the day we wait to board our train at Bangkok's Hua Lamphong railway station. Hoards of humanity press against us as we walk out to our train's platform. Thai passengers waiting for trains to take them to their home provinces to vote tomorrow are not as lucky. There is not enough transportation to handle the unexpected rush of 100,000 people leaving Bangkok by train. Many are left stranded at bus and train stations until the next morning.

March 2, 2000 After thirty hours in transit from the States, I unwind in a Bangkok foot massage parlor. I lie on a bamboo mat while the technician prods each of the foot's pressure points and separately massages each muscle in every direction. Combined with a warmup regimen of stretching and breathing exercises, a foot massage rejuvenates both body and mind, I am told.

It works. I hit the bustling Bangkok streets on foot, absorbing the ambience of the diverse population who enjoy the freedom and tolerance they find in this southeast Asian mecca for alternative lifestyles.

Despite the Thai acceptance of a wide range of opinions, one area that is off-limits to multiple viewpoints is the portrayal of the King. The script for the recent Hollywood movie *Anna and the King* was not government-approved and producers had to film elsewhere. (They chose Malaysia.) When the movie was released, it was banned in Thailand.

January 24, 2000 Ten gunmen from an insurgent group known as God's Army move from the Myanmar jungle across the border into Thailand. They take hundreds of people hostage for twenty-two hours at a hospital in the border town of Ratchaburi. They are demanding that Thailand stop attacks on Myanmar pro-democracy activists who take sanctuary in Thailand. The rebel group in the Myanmar jungle is reportedly led by twin twelve-year-old boys.

The ten gunmen are shot by Thai commandos in a swift pre-dawn raid. Two days later the Myanmar military overruns the jungle base of God's Army and captures fifty people. The fate of the twins is not known.

God's Army is a small fundamentalist Christian splinter band from the Karen National Union, an ethnic group that battles the Myanmar government. The KNU condemns the hospital hostage-taking by God's Army. There are 100,000 Karen refugees in Thailand and 300,000 internally displaced within Myanmar.

October 20, 1999 Speaking at the International Republican Institute's Freedom Award dinner in Washington, D.C., Senator John McCain bestows its 1999 award to Aung San Suu Kyi. Citing the Nobel peace prize winner's "unwavering commitment and courage in the non-violent struggle for democracy and human rights in Burma," he chronicles her lifetime of work. Aung San Suu Kyi, however, is not present at the dinner that honors her. She is in Yangon, Myanmar, a virtual captive in the country she loves. She is afraid to leave.

Earlier this year she made an agonizing choice. The military government refused to grant her cancer-stricken husband a visa to come to Myanmar and visit her for the last time before his death. Political events had caused them to be apart since 1995, but they each accepted the sacrifice that service to her people meant. Instead of the requested visa, the generals offered to let Aung San Suu Kyi leave Myanmar. But there was no guarantee that she would be let back in. Suspicious of a trap, she remained in Myanmar and held a simple Buddhist memorial service upon receiving word that her husband had died on his fifty-third birthday.

May 21, 1999 A thirty-year-old computer geek launches an internet web site at www.gwbush.com which parodies George W. Bush's actual campaign web site. The satirical site is nearly identical in style to the politician's. The tone, however, is markedly different. There is a fabricated image of Bush sniffing cocaine through a straw. There are "news" items about the presidential candidate's plans "to free all 'grown ups' from federal prisons."

The Bush legal office tries to get the site closed down. Failing that, they bring the site owner before the Federal Election Commission, claiming that he must register as a political committee. The lawyers are not successful in stomping on First Amendment rights guaranteeing free speech.

Speaking at a press conference in Austin, Texas, an infuriated Governor Bush declares, "There ought to be limits to freedom."

August 26, 1988 Having arrived back in her home country after living overseas for two decades with her British diplomat husband and children, Aung San Suu Kyi finds a premonition coming true. She is called upon to serve her people. Standing before a half million people at the Shwedagon Pagoda in Rangoon, Burma, she electrifies the crowd with her charismatic speech.

A nineteen-year-old university student, Khan Yang Hu, joins his classmates and marches on the streets of Rangoon to press for political change. As mass protests sweep the country in the following months, Aung San Suu Kyi addresses approximately a thousand more public gatherings. She faces down soldiers with weapons poised. Khan Yang Hu's classmates are shot, arrested, imprisoned and tortured. Some escape and go to Thailand. The universities are shut down. Thousands of other civilians are massacred during the pro-democracy demonstrations.

October 26, 1967 Flying an A-4 fighter jet over North Vietnam, a thirty-one-year-old Navy pilot is suddenly forced to eject himself from the aircraft. He falls to the ground breaking both arms and his right knee. A crowd rushes to him and breaks his shoulder and stabs him in the groin with a rifle bayonet.

The young pilot is taken to the Hai Lo Prison where the French once chained and sometimes guillotined the Vietnamese revolutionaries who fought for freedom from the colonial regime. American pilots who are now captured and held here during the Vietnam War, however, call it the Hanoi Hilton.

The guards refuse to allow the young pilot medical treatment unless he reveals military information and confesses to being a war criminal. But then they discover he is the son of John S. McCain, commander-in-chief of the Pacific fleet. If he denounces America, he can receive medical treatment.

He refuses. Then they offer him an early release but it doesn't include the other American prisoners. He refuses that offer also, and spends the next five-and-a-half years in prison suffering for his beliefs in democratic ideals.

Approximately 500 B.C. Sidhartha Gautama, who later becomes known as The Buddha, lives and teaches in the mountainous northern provinces of India. The word "Buddha" means a Supremely Enlightened One who has obtained the level of the ultimate truth. The Buddha rejects the notion of class distinctions and killing in any form, and expounds the doctrine of equality among humans.

Buddhism is preached in the native languages and develops an extensive monastic and missionary system. These early assemblies of Buddhists establish a method of self governance to preserve order and dignity. A member initiating business does so by making a motion which is then open to discussion. If there is a difference of opinion, a vote is taken by ballot and the matter is decided by the majority.

From India, Buddhism spreads into Burma and throughout southeast Asia.

summer

11. the earth people

BY AIR…

They don't have ordinary names like "Bob" or "Carol." Nor do they live in ordinary houses. They have names like "True" and "Savitri" and they rise out of the ground at dawn when our hot-air balloon floats over their dwellings near Taos, New Mexico.

"I was meditating," Savitri says, her gray locks pulled into a pony tail that swings to the side as she stumbles into the wicker basket for an impromptu tethered ride, "when I heard a dog barking."

The propane burner whooshes and we float upwards again. "Did you come through the gorge?" she asks. The early morning sun still casts a reddish glow over the stark clay forms dotting the sagebrush landscape, and we momentarily drift above this netherworld that lies somewhere between the Flintstones' town of Bedrock and the Jetsons' city of the future.

Too remote to connect to the power grid, Savitri and her neighbors are building "earth ship" homes, she explains. Carved into the ground, their structure is supported by a framework of recycled tires and cans, plastered into a quasi-adobe architecture. Bottles cemented together let in light. Water trickles from the roof into collection vessels. Solar panels recharge batteries.

Covered with mud most likely forfeited by his future home, Jonathan trades places with Savitri, and rises too. His dog, Dexter, the culprit who drew attention to the billowing monster invading his world, suddenly whimpers and stares in bewilderment as his master is whisked upward. We are friendly aliens in this universe, however, and politely return him before moving on to our next adventure.

BY LAND...

We descend into the earth. We follow the pungent trail of sagebrush that tumbles over the edge of the gorge cut into the flat plain by the Rio Grande. The trailhead at La Junta Point quickly disappears above our heads as we step down the gorge's dry gravelly path, assisted by a system of metal stairs and rails that cling to the vertical walls and punctuate the incongruity of our presence. Our trekking party spreads out and criss-crosses down the steep slope like an army of ants in slow motion.

In a level patch of prickly pear cactus, we join forces with a pack of llamas who will carry our provisions for the rest of the trip through the gorge. Saddle bags draped over their midsections, the docile beasts move gingerly down the rock-strewn trail.

"The wind in the canyon does wonderful things among the trees," Patty accurately forecasts from under the sombrero that protects her fair skin from the hot sun. The storm clouds and droplets of rain that threatened the beginning of our hike have skirted the gorge. Our sunny haven knows no dark clouds or strife.

We've all just met. We talk about our own lives and we talk about the earth. "I'd love to have a little more land," Patty, a Taos resident, yearns as some of us lag behind to savor the vanilla-scented whiffs that the crackly bark of the Ponderosa pines surrenders, "but philosophically I have a problem. If everyone has to own ten acres, public land will disappear."

We tug on our lead ropes and the llamas obediently follow our steps as we form a caravan along the floor of the gorge. Passing under tall pines that cast dappled shade, we listen to the soothing rhythm of the Rio Grande coursing its way to the sea. The boulders strewn along our route contain petroglyphs ancient symbols etched into the rock – reminding us that others have come before us.

BY WATER...
Reddish brown waves churn against the sides of the raft as we wedge our wet-suit booties between the floor and tubular sections to prevent ourselves from falling overboard. We sweep past towering basalt cliffs on our way through the "Taos Box."

"You'll know how hard to paddle," Cisco booms from the vessel's center position where he instinctively pushes and pulls the mounted oars in sync with each wave, "by the tone of my voice."

The occupants on the right side of the raft back paddle while those on the left side paddle forward. Then we reverse the pattern. As if we were riding inside a huge washing machine with foaming detergent, we bob haphazardly through a four-mile stretch of river.

"It snowed three feet in the mountains yesterday. The river's running fast." He should know. He's been running the river since his boyhood when he tied inner tubes together and set himself adrift. Today, the perpetual adolescent with tinges of gray in his beard wears Nikon sunglasses, a beaver felt hat, and a T-shirt depicting an overturned raft underneath a caption that says "Rubber Death."

He knows each section of the river, each rock, each wave, by heart. The rapids all have names, sometimes spawned from the events or casualties that occurred in them. We cascade jubilantly over the "ski jump." We cavort through the "rock garden."

We hurtle into a narrow chute framed by jagged rocks taunting us from all angles.

"Back paddle! Back paddle! Harder! Harder!" Cisco screams.

We haven't heard this tone before, and like frightened puppies, we obey. The raft careens past the rocks unscathed and drops into a swirling eddy, bending in the middle as we're sucked downward. The rubber springs back into shape, we pop to the surface, and Cisco cackles with delight.

Fueled by the energy and confidence of a man who's spent his life on the river, we relish each splash of icy cold meltwater on our sun-baked skin.

ACROSS TIME...

We pay our entrance, parking and camera fee, and stroll among the Pueblo Indians' adobe dwellings preserved in a living museum village where tribal members inhabit their ancestral surroundings.

"We don't allow electricity or plumbing," our Native American guide, Blue Lake Flower, says, standing at the edge of a cemetery, "because power and water lines would disturb the spirits who are resting here."

We walk across a courtyard of several acres where the earth once sustained the grain and vegetables that fed the residents. We enter a small chapel.

"Our native religion is based on respect for nature," Blue Lake Flower recites. "But about ninety percent of the tribe also practices the Catholic religion." She points out that the central figure at the church's altar is not Jesus, but rather the Virgin Mary, who symbolizes Mother Earth.

"Each year all healthy adult tribal members make the ceremonial trek to the sacred Blue Lake to renew themselves spiritually. We believe that our ancestors rose from these waters."

We snap pictures, wander on our own, and explore the village's outer adobe wall that represents the barrier between the modern and traditional cultures. Beyond the rows of mud-and-straw adobe houses that rim the open space, the Sangre de Cristo mountain range glistens white against the intense blue sky. And as we drive away in our automobiles, no one will ever convince us that people don't continue to spring from the earth.

12. a mountain biker's karaoke

By the time I had heard choir melodies rolling over emerald hills, listened to ghost stories in eighteenth-century farm houses, and heard school children's voices echoing through medieval castles perched above the sea on my route to northern Wales, I knew. There was no mistaking a native Welsh accent with that of an Englishman.

When I met my guide in Beddgelert Forest for a day of mountain biking, however, all that changed.

"Iorwerth Jones. You can't get any more Welsh than that," the young man introduced himself with a proper English accent that was definitely not Welsh.

Buckling my helmet's strap beneath my chin, I tried rolling the first "r" with some success, but decided that his one-syllable nickname "Ioz" was linguistically neutral.

"People don't believe I'm Welsh. My father is Welsh and my mother is English."

"Ah, that explains it," I said, straddling the lightweight, carbon-fiber frame. I had done a fair amount of road biking with my hybrid, but this was my first time on a mountain bike. I slipped my hands into a pair of padded gloves with cutout fingers.

"First we'll climb out of the forest. If we're lucky, we might get a good view of Mount Snowdon here." Ioz traced his finger on the map. "Then we'll trundle all the way down this side."

"Is it steep?" I asked.

"My friends think I'm a bit mad. I've been known to go over the handlebars in this part."

"I don't mind getting muddy," I said, not eager to hear if there was a Welsh expression for "wimp out."

CRUNCH, RATTLE AND ROLL...

The fat, knobby tires crunched against the gravelly surface of the carriage road that wound its way through the conifer woodland. The steady whoosh of cool morning air felt refreshing as I worked up a mild sweat while pedaling up the gentle incline. Slowly rising above the forest, we passed vistas of lakes and valleys.

The pitch grew steeper and my feet moved rhythmically in circles. Like riding a purple harp on wheels, I strummed my mobile musical instrument by pressing my thumbs and fingers on the shifting mechanism located on each hand grip. The gears harmoniously clicked into place, while the whistle of a steam train inching along the spine of Mount Snowdon toward its misty peak punctuated the symphony.

Soon I found myself looking down a broad, grassy valley. Approximately midway between the ridge and the valley floor, a thin ribbon of rutty trail traversed the open hillside. I coasted a few bike-lengths behind Ioz's lead.

"Keep your peddles level through the mud," he shouted.

The advice worked as I jounced in and out of mucky depressions in the trail while picking up speed. I steered around rocks and away from ledges while careening down the mountain.

A waterfall paraded down the jagged wall of the valley and transformed itself into a gentler ditty inches beneath my sneakers. As if caught inside the song, I entered the stream and cruised through.

At the bottom of the valley we snacked on flapjacks – homemade granola bars with cherries – and sipped water from our bike bottles. Energy restored for the next verse, we hummed over narrow, two-lane highway alongside tangled hedgerows and moss-covered stone fences. Past the Snowdon ranger station, up we climbed again, laboriously scaling the grassy hillside over zig-zagging dirt trails.

Pausing frequently to catch my breath with Ioz patiently waiting, I finally reached the ridge. The secluded Maesgwn

Valley lay in front of us. A chorus of sheep sang out the blues and I chimed in with my own rendition of the mellifluous "bah... bah... bah..." that hung in the rich atmosphere.

The path down the mountain was wider, the pitch steeper, and the surface smoother. A three-foot-high stone wall ran along the right-hand side of the trail, separating ourselves from a sharp drop-off into grass and brambles. Like a precisely composed Mozart sonata whose tempo varies with each movement, we rolled along the life-sized musical staff that stretched over the landscape for miles. I gently squeezed the brakes of my bike to control the song's speed. First allegro... slow it down to allegretto... now andante... back to allegro. Forming the complex bars of our musical score, fuzzy balls of sheep dotted the ribbon everywhere, the clumps of notes quickly scattering as we zipped by. We rounded a bend in the trail and one startled sheep, losing its footing and tumbling down the hill, added a discordant sound to the composition.

We rolled down the path passing empty sheep folds, the stone wall pens where farmers would herd their flocks for shearing. Gliding past an abandoned house, I imagined the lilting Welsh hymns of yesteryear seeping from the cracks of the crumbling stone.

Soon we dropped through populated areas, past white-washed cottages and country gardens, into the village of Llanberis.

"We could grab lunch at *Pete's*," Ioz recommended. "It's a good 'climber's cafe.' You get a lot of food for the money."

"Sounds perfect," I agreed.

As I attacked my jacket potato and Ioz devoured his "monster omelette" behind the store-front plate-glass window of *Pete's Eats Extreme Rock Cafe*, I watched the bikers, hikers, and mountain climbers come and go. We commented on the Welsh one-upmanship with the popular American *Hard Rock Cafe*, despite the lack of any music whatsoever in the establishment. But no matter. I was already in tune with Wales.

I'd like to buy a vowel, please...

I had a dream.

I was playing the *Wheel of Fortune* in Wales. Pat Sayjak was speaking with a Welsh brogue. Vanna White was looking lovely. The game board had only one word. However, the word had thirty-five letters in it.

It was the final round of the show. But the rules were a little different.

"You can choose two letters and buy a vowel," Pat said. "You have thirty seconds to guess the word. You must pronounce it correctly. The category is 'language.'"

Music started to play in the background. Sheep started to bleat.

"I'll take an 'l' and a 'y,'" I said.

The letters on the board started lighting up. Vanna started to run back and forth flipping them over because it was the older style like the show once used. The clock started to tick.

"Wait!" I cried. "I want to buy a vowel."

"I'm sorry," Pat said. "There aren't any. You have twenty seconds left."

"There must be a vowel," I protested. "Every word has a vowel."

"This is Wales," Pat said. "Ten seconds left."

By this time, Vanna had turned over all the letters. The word contained all l's and y's. All I had to do was say the word.

"Lollipop… lolligag… logarithm…" I stammered, mimicking the sounds of some familiar English words.

"Not even close." Pat was smirking. "Five more seconds.

"Laryngitis… lymphocyte… liquefy… lickety-split… Lillith… Lilliputian… lily-livered…"

The buzzer rang. I woke up. My heart was pounding. I was back home speaking American English.

Oh, man… I hate when that happens.

the beddgelert legend...

The name "Beddgelert" translates from the Welsh as "grave of Gelert" and derives from a tragic story.

Prince Llywelyn decided to go hunting one day and left his faithful dog, Gelert, to watch his baby. When he returned, he found Gelert with blood on his mouth and no signs of the baby. Racing to conclusions, Prince Llywelyn slew the dog in a merciless rage.

Suddenly the prince heard cries from underneath a cart and saw a blood-stained wolf skulking around it. The baby was fine, but the simultaneously relieved and heartbroken prince realized he had just killed his trustworthy companion who had actually been protecting the baby by fighting off an attacking wolf. Prince Llywelyn created a gravesite to memorialize Gelert, and since that time the village and surrounding forest came to be known as Beddgelert.

13. where have all the flowers gone?

"Have you got your saddle bags down yet?" the ranch owner asked as we sipped coffee on the dewy porch of the 150-year-old Adirondack camp. Like kids caught without their homework, my four friends and I looked at each other blankly.

"Well, you've got a choice," he teased. "You can bring 'em down, or take the horses upstairs."

Deciding the first option would be easier, I finished placing my camera gear in the long center bag and stuffed the extra jeans and T-shirt around it. Sneakers and toiletries went into the smaller attached side bags. The whole kit would hang over the horse's rump, just behind the saddle.

Although I had just met my traveling companions, I felt as if we shared a common bond that transcended the overnight horse packing journey we'd be making together into the Cold River wilderness, one of the most remote parts of New York State.

I placed my left boot into the left stirrup of my horse's saddle, and grabbing the horn, hoisted my weight over the elegant chestnut-colored Appaloosa with a silvery mane.

The beauty and elegance that were easy to appreciate at ground level, however, diminished with increasing altitude. I felt as if I were sitting on top of a clunky refrigerator balanced on four wobbly stilts. But unlike stilts, these spindly posts bent and moved – all under another entity's control. I wondered how this was going to work.

"Pretend you're holding an ice cream cone." Wrangler Mary Benson arranged the leather reins so the two lines ran through my closed fist. Each line was attached to opposite sides of a metal bit in the horse's mouth. "Then turn your hand either right or left when you want to turn. Pull back when you want to stop."

Seemed simple enough. "What's my horse's name?" I asked.

"This is Flower Girl."

"I call her Flower Child." Our other wrangler, Dave King came over and adjusted the straps on the stirrups so that my legs were almost straight. I assumed he was talking about the horse. But I wondered if his comment might have applied to Mary when she moved to the Adirondacks in the sixties to ski.

Everyone mounted their horses, and Mary stepped forward with Bear, as we assembled into a loose clump behind her. Like a group of giant bees, we swarmed out of the stable and paddock area, crossed the clearing and left the ranch buildings behind us.

"How old are the horses?" I asked.

"Flower Girl is seven years old," Mary said. "But the others are in their mid teens."

"About our ages in horse years," observed Charlotte, an experienced rider and high school English teacher.

Mary explained, "They make good pack horses because they're a little more settled and docile at middle age."

"Like us," I mumbled, trying to get the flower child to join the neatly spaced line that the other horses obediently formed. If I really had been holding an ice cream cone, the scoops would have fallen into the brown, drought-parched grass lining the trail.

The early morning sun highlighted an undisturbed spider's web stretched across a driveway as we clip-clopped along the two-lane paved road. The horse-shoed hooves created a rhythmic, hollow echo down the corridor of lakeside cottages bearing apt name tags like "Tall Pines."

"How do I make her go faster?" I asked, slightly lagging behind the first four horses.

"Give her a kick," Dave called from the rear where he rode Lucky. He also led Sluggo, a sturdy pack horse who carried additional supplies for our trip.

I jabbed the belly of Flower Girl with the heel of my boot, and indeed, she sped up. She trotted down the road while I bounced up and down in the saddle.

"Pull back if you don't want her to go that fast," Dave said.

I pulled back on the reins and she slowed to a crawl. I kicked her again and she trotted. The flower child's engine had only two speeds: slow and fast.

We crossed the road and entered the forest. Shafts of sunlight wiggled through the treetops and darted among the horses' hooves that shuffled through the narrow channel of powdery, pulverized earth. The horses snorted and swished their feathery tails to keep the occasional deer fly from lighting.

After twenty minutes of riding, we stopped in a small clearing. Sensitive to the discomfort of the lead horse receiving the brunt of the bugs, Mary slathered some insect repellent onto a soft cloth pouch similar to a car wash mitt. She put her hand into the mitt and rubbed it over the outside and inside of Bear's ears. She passed it to the other riders who imitated the ritual.

"It must be interesting traveling and writing about outdoor activities," Bob commented as I jotted a few things in my notebook and stashed it back in my saddle bag.

"Absolutely," I agreed, recalling the many places I'd been to and the different people I'd met.

"How long have you been writing?" Bob finished insect-proofing his horse and passed the mitt to me.

I took the mitt and rubbed it over Flower Girl's ears. "Over twenty years," I said, suddenly noticing the slight arthritic stiffness in my fingers. I had worked hard to get to this point but I still had many more things to do and stories to tell.

"What kind of work do you do?" I asked. Although I always enjoy talking shop with other writers, it was a treat to be the only journalist among people from other walks of life.

"I deliver packages for UPS," he said.

"I'll bet you have some unusual things happen," I prodded.

"Well... I just want out. I'll be able to retire next year." A youthful-looking fifty-five that belied the tired edge to his comment, Bob threw his lanky frame onto Queenie and soon we were all back on the trail again.

Our route narrowed into a tunnel-like opening framed by a dense canopy of hardwoods and hemlocks overhead, and a rocky path underfoot. Whereas the sound of steady trotting on smooth pavement was pleasant and reassuring, the intermittent click of horseshoe and hoof against stone was unnerving. I bobbed in and out of the ruts, distrustful of the dexterity of beasts with five times the weight and twice the number of legs as I.

Nevertheless, we snaked over the rolling terrain for hours. I followed Dave's instructions to lean forward while going uphill and backward while moving downhill. Was it his basketball coaching experience at Paul Smith's college that had produced the vigilant, straightforward demeanor, or was it the demeanor that made him suitable for guiding the younger generation?

"Don't let the horses trot downhill," he quickly admonished when I urged Flower Girl to catch up with the pack.

"If you let her get away with that, she'll keep taking advantage of you," he accurately predicted as the flower child swiped a mouthful of maple leaves at her side.

Meanwhile, I dodged the overhanging vegetation and protruding limbs that the horse easily passed by. I quickly learned that, like a toy removed from an infant's field of vision, anything outside a horse's own space doesn't concern it. This egocentric view of the world serves the individual quite well but in the case of some species such as humans, a broader social consciousness must evolve in order to ensure the survival of the species.

The trail grew steeper and ferns lined its sides. In addition to the sound of the hooves hitting rocks, now I heard them make an eerie squishing and popping sound as they sank ankle-deep in mud and were pulled out. So this was the infamous Mud Mountain we were climbing…

If these horses do this route all the time, then this should be easy, I tried to reassure myself. Yet I couldn't imagine any trickier conditions as we painstakingly ascended several hundred feet elevation through mud, fallen debris, hidden roots and slippery rocks.

Squeezing the saddle's horn and swaying side to side, I precariously maneuvered Flower Girl through the inclined obstacle course, and miraculously she obeyed my commands. Slowly, but not so surely, we slogged our way up the mountain. While we let the sweaty horses rest a few minutes at the top, I breathed my own sigh of relief.

If I thought that we had just made a perilous passage, then the descent down the other more steeply graded side of Mud Mountain was material worthy of a new Sylvester Stallone action movie. Each time Flower Girl's front legs sank into the mud and her head drooped, I envisioned myself flipping over the front. Each time I heard a hoof scrape against a mud-covered rock, I imagined the horse tipping over sideways on top of me.

Eyes focused on the trail ahead, I steered Flower Girl away from an exposed boulder face several feet wide. Had she chosen to step across its angled surface, it would have meant an almost certain tumbling act.

"If your horse starts to fall, pull the reins straight up." Dave's words rang in my mind as Flower Girl suddenly stumbled on a rock and I felt her knees buckle. Without hesitation I pulled upward, rather than back, lifting the horse's head. The advice worked and Flower Girl recovered her balance.

Soon the landscape leveled out, and as we marched uneventfully over smoother ground, I thought I understood how a cowboy might form an emotional bond with his horse. That night, I lay awake a few minutes gazing through the netting of my domed tent at the stars sprinkled between the tips of the pines, and thinking about the next day. I listened to the sound of the horses carrying on. The flower child snorted.

Yes, I knew the return trip tomorrow would be grueling. The distance was exactly the same, we would have to cross Mud Mountain, and we were already tired and sore. But somehow I also knew it would be easier this time around.

14. let the forest come to you

"Fly fishing is more an art than a science," my naturalist guide Dave Mallard said as our canoe drifted peacefully on Noyes Pond in the remote corner of Vermont known as its Northeast Kingdom. "Anyone can drop a line with a worm and catch a fish, but not everyone can fly fish."

My skills that evening proved I was neither scientist nor artist because I was unsuccessful in catching any trout. But his point about art seemed to be underscored by the scene that unfolded around us. The excursion from the doorstep of Seyon Ranch had started out gray and drizzly, but by the time we had paddled to the center of the pond we had already immersed ourselves in a palette that would have made Matisse envious.

Bands of neon light brushed the moody, dark hills that encircled the pond while white-tailed deer crept out of the forest to sip at its edge. A beaver swam, ducklings tailgated their mother, and a kingfisher dove from the sky. Clouds highlighted with multi-hued shades of pink tumbled over each other in a race to the sunset.

The water itself, however, is always the focal point of any fisherman's concentration. Patterned strips rippled alongside perfectly glassy patches. I saw intermittent surface blips inside widening concentric circles and concluded that the next morning's breakfast was just moments away. The theory behind fly fishing, I had just learned, is that insect eggs deposited in the muddy lake bottom hatch out and rise to the surface. On the insects' ascent, feeding trout go after them. Sometimes the fish even break through the water surface in their quest to snap up a tasty morsel.

The job of the fly fisherman is to duplicate the look and motion of the insects. This is not an easy task. First, there are infinite styles of commercial and hand-made flies available to mimic the various naturally occurring stages in an insect's life. Something that entices the fish one day may be totally ineffective the next. Second, the fisherman must make the fly move realistically.

As part of my crash course in fly fishing, I received a lesson in casting. Dave explained the "11:00 - 2:00 rule." My arm should extend no further than these clock positions when powering up and releasing the line. The momentum built up and the weight of the lure carries the hook once released.

"The farther you cast, the better," Dave said.

"Why is that?"

"Not only are trout easily spooked by noise," he answered, "but you'll need to re-cast less often."

I fumbled around with my rod and line, but quickly got the hang of it. I noticed that a good cast had its own graceful sound distinguishing it from the briefer whiz and plop of a poor cast. Conversation faded and we soon settled into the rhythmic whoosh-whoosh of our rods whipping through the air. The tranquility of the act, rather than the intended end product was the reward. When we no longer had enough light to see the fishing line, we paddled back to shore.

The other wildlife that I would pursue in the Northeast Kingdom would be through my camera's lens, and would prove only slightly less elusive.

"Let the forest come to you," Dave had told me during our hike to the summit of Big Deer Mountain. If you stand quietly in one spot for thirty minutes, he explained, the animals forget you're there. Soon they will come all around you.

Indeed, on a hike to Peacham Bog we heard the calls of the hermit thrush, oven bird, black-throated green warbler and chickadee. From a canoe, we shared Osmore Pond with a nesting pair of loons who dove under the water and a minute later resurfaced in a different part of the lake. Everywhere I turned there was wildlife, or evidence of it. Dave identified moose scat on the Big Deer trail. On a late-afternoon stroll around Kettle Pond I came upon fresh coyote tracks in a muddy section of the trail close to the water's edge.

For the visitor, the abundance of wildlife in Vermont is no less than idyllic. However, the conservation management policies have had to balance varied sport, environmental and economic interests in the state. People no longer hunt and trap beavers in the numbers they once did because the fur market is down as a result of vigorous animal rights campaigns. Now damage caused by flooding from beaver dams is actually a concern in some areas.

Bruce Amsden, Information and Education Specialist with Vermont's Department of Forests, Parks and Recreation, cautions that "It's OK at this level, but if you magnify this then maybe you think some kind of control is necessary."

Even the numbers of moose have rebounded so strongly in the state that four years ago Vermont opened up moose hunting to sportsmen. In an annual lottery they issue 200 permits for a three-day season. Encouraged by these statistics as well as seeing "moose crossing" signs on the highways, I went on my own photographic moose hunt at dusk one evening. Driving along Route 105 near the Canadian border, I kept my eyes peeled for the beasts in the boggy flats east of Island Pond. Remembering Dave Mallard's advice about letting the animals come to you, I even parked my car and waited patiently in an area where they were known to be spotted. But wildlife doesn't operate on human time schedules and I had to get back.

According to biologists, a moose has a very small brain. The animals are not known to become habituated to civilization or to otherwise display any intelligent behaviors such as those sometimes exhibited by bears. I never did see a moose during my stay, but maybe they really weren't so dumb. After all, they eluded me for four days and gave me good reason to return to the Northeast Kingdom.

fall

15. the hunted

My question tumbled out as incongruously as the yellow burst of a cottonwood punctuating the dark Ponderosa pines which gave South Dakota's Black Hills their name.

"Are you a cowboy?" I asked our open-air Jeep driver.

His brow furrowed. "No, I'm not a cowboy." Joe, the retired Marine who spoke with a Maine accent considered the notion absurd.

I pointed my camera toward a lone pronghorn antelope prancing over a hilltop. "How'd you come to settle in South Dakota?"

"I lived in California a while." He pulled the vehicle onto the shoulder of the Wildlife Loop Road we had been traveling. "But I wanted a small place. A place with a lot of good hunting and fishing, and some pretty good shopping."

"What do you hunt?"

"Everything."

I clicked the shutter. Like a Pavlovian reflex conditioned by a summer full of tourists' instructions, Joe drove away in search of the next wildlife sighting. This time the vehicle lived up to it's off-road capabilities and we entered a wooded thicket.

"If these oaks have dropped their acorns, we've got a good chance of seeing turkey and deer in here." Even when he wasn't hunting, he was hunting.

We passed through the woods. I wondered if Teddy Roosevelt's footsteps might have trod along the same route in his quest for big game in the Black Hills. Today, the eighty-three-square-mile Custer State Park harbored the elk, mountain goat, bighorn sheep and coyote that state residents could hunt under a permit system, and the buffalo that out-of-state hunters who paid $2,500 for a three-day guided hunt might bag.

Our Jeep climbed the trail and we came to rest on a high knoll at the edge of the forest – a perfect vantage point for marksmen to sight their prey moving across the open prairie. I saw an elaborate system of corrals at the far end of one valley.

"So, this roundup tomorrow," I mused. "That's where the buffalo end up?"

* * *

The next morning a troop of thirty volunteer cowboys and cowgirls, selected by lottery from a pool of nationwide applicants, listened attentively on horseback to their instructions. Their group leaders held up maps dividing the park's hills and valleys into areas of responsibility.

I climbed aboard my own horse: the back of a four-by-four pickup. I was one of several journalists that park management had allowed to ride in the roundup. Under the precisely choreographed plan, the horsemen and women, and motorized rangers with radio communication, would herd the park's approximately 1,400 bison from summer grazing throughout the park to a central location where they would be branded, sorted and vaccinated. As the park lands can only support approximately 900 head, the excess would be auctioned off to ranchers, with the money earned used for the park's activities.

The signal went off and I watched the horses gallop gracefully out of sight. I clung to the ropes and grab bars in the back of the pickup as it careened over park roads and rutty prairie.

Eventually we came to stop near a small stream with hills rising sharply on one side of the valley. Silhouetted against the brilliant blue sky like a scene from an old Western, a line of cowboys moved along the ridge. We sat and waited.

Then the buffalo came. First a group of two or three moved quickly past the pickups which had been strategically parked to funnel the animals in the direction in which they were supposed to travel. Several more groups trotted by. The pace quickened. Soon dozens of beasts galloped single file past me. The 2,000-pound bulls and 1,200-pound cows which looked so docile grazing on the prairie created an entirely different persona as they charged along the stream bed. Having been forewarned that the pickup might need to take off at a moment's notice, I knew their massive power was not a force to be challenged.

The instant the pickup drivers received the radio message that the last buffalo from this area had passed by, we took off once again. Traveling at highway speed over unpredictably spaced hummocks, rocks and holes, we headed for the junction with the adjoining valleys from which other teams would be driving their buffalo. This time there would be no waiting.

When we arrived I saw a wider, flatter terrain. The cowboys and cowgirls were galloping alongside the frenzied beasts. The loosely scattered animals slowly converged into a tighter group, joined by ever-increasing throngs of buffalo from seemingly every direction.

All horses and all vehicles now came into play. We pushed tighter and tighter, moving in tandem with the stampeding herd. I found myself at arm's length from individual bison whose sole attention was fixed ahead.

As the pickup came to the crest of a small hill, the driver barked orders to hold on tightly. The vehicle passed over the top and I lunged forward as it darted down the steep incline. I looked down. Ahead of me I saw a pulsating swarm of energy covering the terrain. We pushed forward into the chocolate sea.

By now the first buffalo were hitting the corrals and I saw clouds of brown dust rise from the earth in front of me. The animals were shunted into various fenced holding areas, their power finally contained.

As the dust settled, the sound of thundering hooves was replaced by the clanging of iron gates. Buffalo passed one by one through the "squeeze chute" where they were weighed, vaccinated, and blood was drawn for testing. The hides of newly born calves received a sizzling stamp which included the last digit of the current year. The yard operation was routine and forceful with adequate human muscle on hand to ensure that the process moved swiftly. There could be no bottlenecks.

When I had seen enough, a Native American teenage worker politely slid a gate open for me at an opportune time when no animal was passing through. Could his tender years see any irony in re-establishing for hunting what hunting had taken away from his ancestors? Later that night I studied the brochure prepared by South Dakota's Department of Game, Fish and Parks.

Bison made their way to America by crossing the ancient land bridge that once connected Asia with the North American continent. Many plains Indian tribes depended on the noble beasts for survival. At their peak, an estimated 60 million bison roamed the plains of North America. By the 1870s, only a few isolated herds remained.

16. these are not mountains

"No, these are not mountains," our naturalist guide flatly denied as I stood atop the summit of Bartolome and studied the adjacent peaks of the other islands in the Galapagos chain. A stiff wind blew bits of volcanic ash against my legs with needle-like sharpness. In the sea below, a flock of miniature penguins swam to shore and scrambled onto the barren, black rocks.

She was right, I decided. On her mainland Ecuador, Cecibel knew mountains that soared 20,000 feet into the sky, were cloaked with ice, and even held entire cities. The Galapagos Islands, baking in the equator's sun six hundred miles from the South American continent, were indeed no match.

I listened to her explanations of lava tubes, lava bombs and lava pools. The words shot out in a rapid-fire Spanish accent with an immediacy that emphasized the relatively young geological age of the islands. Scientific estimates place the oldest of the Galapagos islands at approximately 3.5-5 million years old. Never having had any connection with the continent, the land developed distinctly different forms of life. In his 1835 voyage, Charles Darwin catalogued the unusual species he encountered, and his observations later formed the basis for his revolutionary theories of evolution.

This particular island, however, was devoid of most vegetation except for the ankle-high tiquilia plants colonizing the slopes. Cecibel pointed out that even these pioneer plants, with their fuzzy white hairs to reflect the sun, were uniquely adapted to the harsh environment. My friends and I snaked over the eerie lunar landscape among splatter cones, tuff cones and parasitic cones until we reached the shore where our *panga* waited. The little skiff would shuttle us out to the cruising yacht MY *Letty* anchored in deeper waters. Sleeping and eating aboard the ship, we would spend several days exploring the wildlife and ecology of other islands in the archipelago before moving on to Quito.

"Today will be bird day," our second guide, Maria, announced as we made a "wet landing" and waded through a sparkling turquoise lagoon onto the sandy beach of Genovesa. We were actually inside the crater of an extinct, partially-eroded volcano. The surrounding cliffs that formed the C-shaped bay were the inner walls of the crater's rim, while the base of the volcano extended to the ocean floor.

A group of dark brown sea lions sunned themselves on the beach but made no attempts to move away as we scampered to higher ground. In the Galapagos Islands, the animals had evolved without any mammalian predators and therefore had no fear of humans. In fact, the sea lions were very curious and often approached us as we sat on the beach, walked, or snorkeled in the bays during our twice-daily excursions onto land.

Genovesa had a somewhat denser vegetative cover than Bartolome, but it was still not the lush, green landscape I had expected from a habitat that lies at the same latitude as the Amazon rain forests. I learned, in fact, that the Galapagos Islands have a more temperate subtropical, rather than tropical, climate. The frigid Humboldt current flows north from Antarctica and creates an ecosystem that allows cold-loving penguins and heat-seeking lava lizards to coexist as neighbors. Very little rain falls.

We dried our feet, put on our hiking boots and wandered into the scrubby brush. At arm's length, red-footed boobies stared into my camera with wide-eyed innocence. The turkey-sized birds with colorful webbed feet were once called *bobo* birds, after the Spanish word meaning "fool," because they were so easily duped. Sailors and other early island visitors could simply walk up and grab one to eat.

Maria playfully imitated the boobies' woodpecker-like sound, but then cautioned against touching or otherwise altering any plant or animal. She described the heartbreak of watching helplessly as frigate birds – the "pirates of the air" – attack baby sea turtles making their way into the surf. "We cannot interfere with nature," she said, explaining the national park's philosophy.

That night, however, churning our way through rough seas to the next destination, we felt like vulnerable turtle hatchlings ourselves. I rocked from side to side in my bed while my shipmates in upper cabins tumbled from their bunks onto the floor. In the morning we gladly stepped onto solid ground into the primordial world of Santa Cruz island's "Dragon Hill" region.

Like actors in a Steven Spielberg movie, we hiked through a strange cactus forest with glimpses of volcanic peaks between spiny branches. Were it not for the hot sun and the sweat beading on my brow, I would have thought the transparent crystalline layer covering the trail's red earth was ice. It turned out to be salt, and we passed a brackish pond, entering a secret world where flamingoes poked their heads underwater to find shrimp, and flapped their wings in an exotic courtship dance. Less than 400 individuals of this sub-species existed in the world, and they were found only here in the Galapagos Islands.

The trail climbed through the highlands and we passed barren stands of palo santo trees, also known as "holy stick trees" because they normally flowered at Christmas, and on the mainland, churches burned the woody stems as incense. Soon we spotted a trough-like depression in the loose, sandy soil.

We followed the winding track to the shade of yellow-flowered mujuju bushes where a prehistoric-looking land iguana rested. The mottled yellowish color and scaly coat with ridges, peaks and crest gave it the appearance of a dinosaur, but the reptile was only about the size of a cocker spaniel. Nevertheless, nature had stacked the evolutionary deck in this endemic species' favor by endowing males with two penises. There was a greater chance of reproductive success when the males raped the unwilling females because they could quickly penetrate using the organ in closest proximity.

This theme was repeated with the marine iguanas as well. On Santiago, I watched clusters of grotesque black creatures swarm over seaside cliffs with the same color and rough texture as their skin. As if their appearance and behavior weren't disgusting enough, these animals had evolved the propensity to spit. This action was a mechanism to rid the body of the excess salt from a diet of algae.

I hiked along the rocky shore and stepped carefully across an arched bridge that waves had carved from the black lava. The protected grottos and ledges contained fur sea lions, a species distinct from the more common sea lions that lived along flatter shore areas. The fur sea lions had longer fins that allowed them to better climb among the rocks. They fished at night, except during the full moon when they might fall victim to sharks.

High visibility was no problem for the bright orange, tough-shelled crabs that scurried across the rocks and clung to nooks and crannies bathed by the foamy tide. I watched these Sally

Lightfoot crabs constantly shift position as I contemplated the metaphor of the name's origin. As one story goes, Sally, the lover of an early Galapagos settler, had an unchanging menu of crabmeat until one day she became bored with the crabs, her boyfriend and her lifestyle, and decided to leave.

It was soon time for us to leave and I did so reluctantly, thinking how the few days I had spent in the Galapagos Islands could not do justice to the incredible diversity that took evolutionary processes millions of years to bring about. As our boat passed Leon Dormido at sunrise, I watched blue-footed boobies circle the vertical volcanic cone that had been dramatically split in two. With goodbye hugs from Cecibel and Maria, I felt a bit sad. But I also looked forward to tomorrow when I would see the real mountains of the Andes range.

The air was chilly and I still felt a bit light-headed from the rapid increase in altitude. At 9,200 feet, the bustling streets of Quito lay before me, while thick clouds hung against the series of peaks circling the city. A mix of high rises and tile-roofed stucco buildings stretched through the Valley of Tumbaco.

"We're entering now to the old part of the city," said Marco, our guide for the day. As a writer, I detected occasional grammatical slips in his English. But Marco was college-educated and this was a very good job in Ecuador where the average income was the equivalent of $120 per month.

I was not prepared to see such poverty. I walked through cobblestone streets and open squares where children scurried to me with outstretched hands. In the morning, bent-over women pawed through garbage bags set at curbside. Girls who were still young enough to be playing with dolls lay on sidewalks clutching tiny bundles that turned out to be real babies. Even as late at 10:00 P.M., children that looked to be only four years old were still in the streets.

Yet despite the country's social problems, there was an unobtrusive dignity. Indians celebrated their heritage by performing a ceremonial demonstration dance in a public square outside a church. A man with a guitar stood in a gas station and serenaded motorists.

Marco described the recent political crisis in which President Bucaram, known to countrymen as *el loco*, was forced out of power in a tense standoff in February 1997. But he bristled at the U.S. State Department's advisory posted on the internet that corruption is endemic to South America.

Throughout my visit to Ecuador, I tried to sift through the curious mix of values and images. This was a country born out of the Spanish conquistadors' search for gold, women and food. But Lorena Bobbitt, the Ecuadorian woman who single-handedly destroyed that machismo image, was now a national heroine.

My friends and I strolled down one street with no less than seven churches within a few blocks of each other. Men with shoe-shine kits sat in front of newsstands displaying the porno mag *Mango* side by side with Princess Diana memorial issues. A few steps away, at the church of St. Augustin, monks reverently filed past intricately carved cedar mouldings. I studied stained glass windows in the church of el Sagrario.

Candles flickered and organ music played inside the church of St. Francis as I tiptoed up the aisle during a mass. It was the middle of the week and the church was filled. People who seemingly had nothing had no poverty of spirit in this church high in the beautiful Andes mountains. Wherever I traveled, they had been quick to smile, lend assistance and offer an embrace. The smell of incense hovering, we lingered a few minutes and then climbed into our shiny van that whisked us away.

We drove to the summit of El Panecillo where a huge statue of the Virgin of Quito overlooked the entire city. The metropolis looked like the pieces of an unassembled jigsaw puzzle scattered among the elongated pattern of mountains and valleys. Patches of blue sky, clouds and shadows swirled together until suddenly and magically the pieces of the puzzle fell into place. At once, I knew that whether it was old or geologically new, desolate or lavishly biodiverse, poor or rich, lowlands or "real" mountains, Ecuador was all a matter of one's perspective.

17. safe passages

On Tuesday, September 11, 2001, New York State residents Cliff and Penny Cool received a double blow. During a leisurely boating vacation in Ontario province under sunny blue skies, the news that shocked the world crackled over the radio in their cabin cruiser.

As most of us did that morning of the terrorist attacks, they tried to contact loved ones to make sure they were safe. But the Cools had special cause for concern. One son was a commercial airline pilot. The other worked in lower Manhattan.

With phone lines overloaded and cell phone reception unavailable in the remote area, the Cools decided to navigate their boat back to the States. They would pilot the craft through a system of interconnected waterways – the historic Rideau Canal – back to their home in Henderson Harbor on the New York shore of Lake Ontario.

I met the Cools passing through the Beveridges Lockstation in the Rideau Canal where I was also positioned that fateful week. I was exploring its lakes, rivers, channels and waterside villages with an itinerary that combined both driving and boating. I had no clue that their history would have any relevance to the modern-day history that was about to unfold.

I had begun my trip September 9th in Kingston, the site of a Loyalist settlement after the Revolutionary War. When I arrived, the small city on the northern shore of Lake Ontario reminded me of a Martha's Vineyard without the attitude. The busy harbor, three local universities, and historic downtown district formed a playful mix that drew tourists from many countries as well as from Canada itself. I felt connected and safe as people of all ages and nationalities bustled about.

I ate dinner in an Italian sidewalk cafe, sipped my morning coffee in an English pub, had lunch in a Greek bistro, and strolled along the shore walk, a well marked pedestrian and bicycle path that winds through the city and maintains continuous access to the water.

On September 10th I toured Bellevue House, an Italianate villa which served for a brief period as the home of Sir John A. Macdonald, Canada's first prime minister. Macdonald envisioned a confederation of all provinces – a unit functioning for the benefit and protection of everybody while retaining individual cultural identities and freedoms – that would become the Canada we know today. Had he known that his idea would continue to serve a broader world vision centuries later? Had he anticipated that its very principles would be challenged?

Then I traveled north from Kingston toward Ottawa, loosely following the path of the 125-mile-long Rideau Canal. After the War of 1812, the British had feared an attack by Americans on the St. Lawrence River. They wanted to develop an alternate route to Kingston completely out of enemy range. Connecting the abundant natural lakes and rivers with a canal system would provide a secure inland water route from Ottawa to Kingston. They commissioned Colonel By and his Royal Engineers who would design the system of fifty locks.

Dwarfed by the massive wooden gates which are still opened and closed by lock attendants who hand crank the "crab" winches, my boat gracefully bobbed up or down the sandstone chambers as water rushed in or out. I glided past golden fields and forests tinged with autumn colors. Two-lane roads wound through the valleys and occasionally crossed the river beds with an iron- or wooden-deck bridge.

During the construction years, however, life on the canal was not so idyllic. Many immigrants and other citizens faced backbreaking labor and bouts of malaria to make safe passages for their countrymen. Thousands died.

Once the canal was in operation, one's guard still had to be kept up. At the remote Jones Falls site I watched a blacksmith re-enact the processes that allowed lockstations to maintain their seamless operation. After all, if a single cog in one lock failed, the whole system broke down. At the top of the multi-lock hill, I toured the "defensible lockmaster's house." Peering out of gun holes in the thick stone masonry walls, I imagined the uneasiness his family lived under from day to day. Their life required constant vigilance should the unthinkable happen.

Although the anticipated attack from America in the 1800s never materialized, almost 200 years later the unthinkable did happen.

"David, you might want to watch this," a staff member said as I entered my hotel after a morning walk around Merrickville, a lockside artisans' village of historic Ontario farmhouse-style homes. She directed me toward a TV screen where the events were unfolding in front of blank stares.

I couldn't look away, and yet I couldn't absorb the information. It wasn't real. It didn't make sense. Strangely, I felt nothing. The U.S.-Canadian border crossings were immediately closed and I needed time to process, so I decided to stay and continue my trip. Although the locks near Ottawa, the Canadian capital, were evacuated for security precautions, I visited additional lockstations south of the city. But I saw them differently now. They became more than just structural curiosities for tourists.

The channels and locks were the instruments that today would ironically provide safe passage for Americans whom they were designed to protect against. Now there was a different breed of invader who attacked not just my country but the entire world when it slammed airplanes into buildings. When the dust settled, both figuratively and literally, the principles of freedom would need a new type of canal to offer safe passages for all people.

When I arrived home myself, I was still numb but I knew the story I had to tell would not be complete until I reported on the outcome of the American couple. I called and spoke with Penny Cool who told me she and her husband had made it home safely. Their pilot son was not flying on September 11th. Their other son, who would have been working in lower Manhattan when the attacks occurred, had just changed jobs and was now uptown. Although I didn't know either son and had only made the briefest of acquaintances with the parents, I breathed a sigh of relief when I hung up the phone.

And then I finally cried. I cried for all those who did not find safe passages back home that day.

18. crossings

If I had been a song, I couldn't have struck a more discordant note among the lute and mandolin music that filled the air in Marakesh, Morocco. I was clearly a westerner – but not a dashing Indiana Jones darting through the spice-filled markets and overturning donkey-driven carts. Wearing sneakers, nylon jogging pants and a day pack, I wandered among the exotic mix of people and cultures.

"'Scuse me, sir. Hello, sir." A man carrying leather belts walked alongside me. "I want to be your friend."

Inside the maze-like *souk* (marketplace), booths selling leather goods, rugs, fabrics, silver and ceramics competed for my attention while numerous such "friends" attached themselves to me like a bad case of static cling. Just when I thought I had ripped free on one corner, they would only reappear around the next.

"You like this? No? What color you like?"

Nevertheless, I enjoyed the game. Morocco had been the crossroads of many civilizations throughout history and I was seeing bits and pieces unfold in front of me. About forty percent of the nation's current population is Berber, a tribe of people who, as one theory states, may have migrated from central Africa. Islamic civilizations had spread into the area from the East. Commercial caravan routes developed and became conduits for rock-salt, gold and other prized items. The intensified trade between northern Africa and Spain required the construction of stop-over cities including Marakesh. And in the 1970s, trade of a different sort – drugs – was legendary.

Even today the *souk* had a secretive air as spice dealers waved open vials of saffron and other mid-eastern spices under my nose while beckoning me to step into their cubicles of commerce. Blending just as easily into the hub-bub and crowd, two young men walked hand in hand, unconcerned about enjoying each other's touches. Out in the open square, cobras and other snakes reared mysteriously from carpets laid on the ground while snake charmers played haunting melodies.

I had arrived here only that morning from an entirely different world...

CROSSING OVER

As bright as the moon in the clear Arabian night, the "white city" of Agadir glistened on southern Morocco's Atlantic coast. Before dawn broke, I left the gates of the resort complex where Italians, Germans and increasingly more Americans flocked for sunny winters. Nearly half came to play golf on the irrigated private grass of local courses, or to enjoy other leisure sports. Leveled by an earthquake in 1961, the city had been rebuilt and now tourism formed nearly a third of the economy (led by fishing and agriculture).

While the starry night slowly faded into morning, my friends and I sleepily jounced inside the comfortable van making our way over the 250-kilometer route toward Marakesh. Shadowy layers of hills emerged into red striations and the world outside grew brighter around each hairpin turn. But like the diamond shapes on entry doors to ward off the evil eye in the mud, straw and stone Berber houses, my glass shield would not let me contaminate that space with western ways. These were isolated worlds, never mixing. And if we dared to try, the distant, jagged mountains lining the horizon like a mouthful of neglected teeth would bite these intruders and spit them back from where they came. We moved on.

Alongside the desolate stretches of mountain road, vessels of oil and honey sat on rickety stands and I wondered where they drew their product or their customers, as sources for neither appeared anywhere in sight. We passed stony, arid fields with prickly pear cacti and indigenous argon trees that entice a unique species of tree-climbing goat to feed on their branches. On larger, cultivated plains groves of olive and citrus trees flourished in the sun.

The sun now hit the sides of the mountains forming perfect geometric angles of light and shadow between the folds. I would see these same triangles repeated in the designs of the architecture, clothing and artifacts throughout Morocco. Islamic law precluded any flowers, animals or human body parts from being represented in artwork because only God could give life to an image.

Soon we drove through villages and from my roving bubble I watched clusters of men dressed in dark brown robes with pointy hoods move in tandem with us. Wearing the traditional *gellabas*, they were congregating in the *souks* to do their shopping. Women stayed at home. Not unlike the days of harems (the word actually means a place reserved for women, rather than the women themselves), a Berber man might have two or three wives waiting at home for him.

And yet, I learned of the inevitable social changes that come with exposure to outside influences. In 1995, Islamic law was amended to require the consent of a man's first wife when he wanted to marry a second. The official languages of Morocco – Arabic and French – would soon become Arabic and English. Not all trends were permanent, however. After a period of westernized dress, women were reverting back to traditional Islamic clothes. During my stay in Morocco, I would see figures draped from head to toe in flowing silk cloth. Their mysterious, dark eyes would shun my glances and the very sight of my camera would send them scurrying in another direction.

When their defenses were down, or perhaps when they felt less threatened, the women's constraint wasn't as evident. On a land rover excursion across the desolate dunes of southern Morocco's desert, we had been amused by the antics of three animated women who danced and waved back at our distant greetings. Why had I assumed that a covered body was necessarily shy? If I could crack through barriers and get closer, I might have some clues about this hidden society. But the cultural walls that humanity erected around itself sometimes seemed as impenetrable as the physical ones surrounding the ancient fortified *kasbas* I saw dotting the hills.

Later that morning we crossed over the Marakesh city limits and passed through the gates from the new city into the old walled city. I recalled all these diverse images of people and places as I walked through the winding byways where rules and stereotypes seemed to vanish in the crowds.

It all seemed so natural, and yet so difficult.

index

An index of people, places, plants, animals, activities and foreign terms

Beaver, 49, 53, 54, 117, 120

Beddgelert, 101, 108

Bedrock, town of, 95

Bees, killer, 1

Belize, 69-77

Benson, Mary, 110, 111

Berber, 146, 147, 148

Berkshire mountains, 2

Beveridges Lockstation, 139

Bicycling, 1, see also
Mountain biking

Big Deer Mountain, 119

Big Deer trail, 120

Birch, 45

Bird, 40, 49, 69, 119, 132

Black Hills, 125-129

Black-throated green
warbler, 119

Blanco, Cape, 57, 58

Blue Lake, 100

Blue Lake Flower, 99

Bobbitt, Lorena, 137

Bobo bird, see Boobie

Bog Pond, 56

Boobie, 133, 136

Boston, 79

Bothnia, Gulf of, 33

Bradley, Bill, 83

Breccia cliffs, 24, 26

Britain, 71, see also England

Brooklyn, 42

Brown, Margaret Wise, 17

Brown, Murphy, 8

Bucaram, President, 137

Buckley, Mr., 71, 72

Buddha, Buddhist, 83, 85, 87,
90, 92

Buffalo roundup, 126-129

Burma, see Myanmar

Bush, George W., 83, 90

Butterfly, blue morpho, 77

By, Colonel, 141

Cactus, prickly pear, 96, 147

California, 2, 62, 63, 81, 83,
84, 125

Camden, 82

Canada, 12, 37, 43-50, 72, 120,
139-142

Canoeing, 53-56, 117, 119

Caracol, 71

Carr, Carolyn, 69

Catskill Mountains, 37-42

Cattle, 60

ABOUT THE AUTHOR

David Lee Drotar is the award-winning author of six books including *Hiking: Pure and Simple*, the first complete book devoted exclusively to hiking.

ALSO BY THE AUTHOR:

- Pocket Calculators: How To Use And Enjoy Them
  (with Arnold Madison)
- Fun Science
- Microsurgery: Revolution In The Operating Room
- Hiking: Pure & Simple
- Hiking The U.S.A.: A Sourcebook For Maps,
  Guidebooks & Inspiration
- The Fire Curse And Other True Medical Mysteries

"Drotar's inner messages on life often make you reflect on who you are and what you're doing with yours. It's a book that I could read over and over again and each time immerse myself into a scene that many of us only dream about feeling, tasting and believing."

– Posted on Amazon.com by Kelly M. Becker